DIA
LOG
UES

— ON —

SEXUALITY

SPARK
HOUSE

Printed in the United States

25 24 23 22 21 20 19 1 2 3 4 5 6 7 8

ISBN 9781506453828

Written by Isaac Archuleta, Carla Ewert, Rev. Marcus Halley, Linda Kay Klein, George Mekhail. Brandi Miller, Dr. Tina Schermer Sellers, Rev. Dr. Paula Stone Williams
Edited by Carla Barnhill
Cover design by Joe Reinke
Art Direction by Joe Reinke
Interior Design by Joe Reinke

DIALOGUES ON SEXUALITY

Sparkhouse team: Carla Barnhill, Aaron Christopher, Julie Coffman, Leigh Finke, Erin Gibbons, Kristofer Skrade, Josh Stifter, Jeremy Wanek, Erik Ullestad

Library of Congress Cataloging-in-Publication Data is available

PUBLISHED BY SPARKHOUSE
510 Marquette Avenue
Minneapolis, MN 55402
wearesparkhouse.org

TABLE OF CONTENTS

FOREWORD

BY ROBERT T. FLYNN

I started coming out as a gay man in the late 1980s when I was a twenty-year-old undergraduate. It was clear to me that if I wanted my friends and family to know and even share my hopes and dreams, they needed to know who I was and who I would love. Unfortunately, the fundamentalist faith community my family was a part of played a negative role in this process—as religious communities often have—and I walked away from the church.

But I didn't walk away from religion. In fact, I remained fascinated by how belief systems shape the way people see the world. I developed an interest in biblical criticism and church history and, ultimately, majored in religion and went on to earn a graduate degree from a divinity school.

My family couldn't understand my decision to study religion when, from their perspective, I had rejected Christianity by coming out. They assumed the church would continue to reject me and that I was setting myself up for disappointment. I admit, I shared some of those fears. But as I studied religion in graduate school, I met people who were both deeply Christian and who loved me as a gay man. I started attending an Episcopal congregation that had an intentional ministry to gay men. In class, in church, and in the library, I learned I could experience the love of Christ in ways that fundamentalist Christianity had never shown me—through the liturgy, the sacraments, and the community. These practices helped reconstruct a faith that was based not on a narrow interpretation of the Bible but on the centering power of the gospel message and the community of believers gathered around the table.

While completing my master's degree in 1994, I met and fell in love with the man who would later become my husband. Guy was finishing his PhD and working in a Lutheran congregation. As a gay man, Guy was barred from ordination. Nonetheless, his deep commitments to Lutheran theology and tradition were too strong to let the policies of the church push him away. Those policies were, however, enough to make me leery, and I continued to worship at the Episcopal congregation that had made my return to the church possible. When we moved to California in 2000, we found a welcoming Lutheran congregation where we could worship together openly as a couple, and I joined the Lutheran church.

One benefit of coming out was that I gained the ability to see the world from a different point of view. The books I read, the people I met, and even my own experiences as an openly gay man brought to light the profound gender assumptions that run underneath so much of the way the world works. This knowledge was a gift to me. It helped me reframe experiences I'd had as a child, when any signs of femininity in myself or other young boys were quickly sniffed out. I learned at an early age that to show such "weakness" was to risk ridicule and punishment. I learned how sexist stereotypes limit girls and women, how gendered expectations put roadblocks in their path, and how patriarchy endangers the physical safety and wholeness of anyone who isn't perceived to be a straight, cisgender male. At the same time, I learned how these very same stereotypes had given me—and continue to give me—unearned privilege. As a man, I reap the benefits of favorable assumptions about my competence. I have a leg up in nearly every institutional setting. My safety can sometimes be at risk because of my sexual identity, but as a white man, I still walk through a world that defers to my maleness more often than not.

The excellent essays in this book offer a chance to see the world from different points of view. The book begins with a powerful chapter on the connections between patriarchy and particular theological perspectives, and how these ideas diminish everyone— including those who benefit from them. The successive essays then offer insight into the effects of patriarchal expectations on women, on marriage, on the lesbian and gay experience, and the experiences of transgender individuals. The authors ask probing questions like: What role do churches play in undergirding or undermining patriarchy? How does a church fully live into its calling by affirming the worth of LGBTQ people? How do we create language and teaching and support around sexuality that creates wholeness instead of shame?

As you read these essays, you might find yourself getting defensive or thinking these perspectives don't relate to you or your church. When that happens—and it's likely to happen, it happened to me—I encourage you to let that tension serve as a signal that you're being presented with a gift, an opportunity to listen and learn. I encourage you to set aside defensiveness and carefully consider the perspectives and information being presented. Receive the experience of others as you would want them to accept your own. If we are to be the body of Christ, if the church is to be a place where people feel God's love and care, then we have to listen to the stories of people who don't feel that love and care. We have to be willing to break down the walls that keep them out, even if they are the same walls that help us feel safe.

I wish I had this book to read as a young person, and I commend it to you and your congregation as a resource for entering into liberating conversations on these topics. In 1 John 4:19 we learn that "We love because [God] first loved us." That verse has always been close to my heart because it affirms God's love for us and shows us that the love of God is the spark for the love we show one another. I encourage you to enter into conversation with the assurance that God loves you, God loves your siblings in Christ, and God loves your neighbor. Take God's love with you into these conversations—and may you be blessed by them!

Robert T. Flynn has worked in scholarly and art publishing for more than twenty years and holds degrees from Haverford College and Yale Divinity School. He is married to the Rev. R. Guy Erwin, bishop of the Southwest California Synod of the Evangelical Lutheran Church in America.

1

A MAN'S WORLD

THE CHURCH AND THE PERVASIVE PROBLEM OF PATRIARCHY

BY BRANDI MILLER

when my mother was pregnant
with her second child, i was four
i pointed at her swollen belly confused at how
my mother had gotten so big in such little time
my father scooped me in his tree trunk arms and
said the closest thing to god on this earth
is a woman's body it's where life comes from
and to have a grown man tell me something
so powerful at such a young age
changed me to see that the entire universe
rested at my mother's feet[1]

– Rupi Kaur

I was sitting across the table from an older couple who were considering financially supporting my ministry. As we talked about student discipleship and ministry structures, I could anticipate the man's question:

"So, who is the head of the ministry and who do you have around you to disciple the men in the community?"

This line of questioning is common in my meetings with men who are considering becoming ministry partners. When women are asked about discipling men, it's a question about authority, about whether women are able, qualified, called, God-permitted, or created to lead in general—let alone to lead men. It's regularly assumed that as a woman, I need men to disciple my students, not because I lack the qualifications, but because my gender inherently makes my discipleship less God-ordained or biblical than that of a male counterpart.

Interestingly, a male coworker whom I supervise was recently asked if he had women discipling the women in his Bible study. But this had nothing to do with his qualifications or authority. No, his donor was concerned about the potential sexual or romantic implications of this cross-gendered discipleship. The donor told my coworker that "anything could happen." And while it is true that having people of the same gender give advice to or disciple each other is sometimes helpful, that was not the foundation of either of these questions.

Instead, these questions reflect the patriarchal assumptions embedded in much of western Protestant theology and practice. Patriarchy, a social system in which men hold power and women are largely excluded from power, creates the context for gender stereotyping, generalizing, exclusion, and abuse in faith spaces that manifest in everyday interactions like mine.

Note, for example, the cultural and often Christian assumption that a mediocre or ill-equipped man is more qualified for or entitled to leadership than a well-qualified woman on the basis of genitalia or gender. There are arguments that say the church is in danger if women lead because of their inherently sexual or emotional presence. In reality, the church under primarily male leadership is currently in crisis, with declining numbers, rampant sexual abuse scandals, and a growing reputation for hypocrisy. For decades, there have been more women attending church than men, while the leadership has remained steadfastly male.[2] This gap is now diminishing, not because more men are attending church, but because fewer women are.

If we believe at a base level what Jesus says about knowing a tree by its fruit, then we need look no farther than the fruit of male-centered leadership in the church and in culture to ask whether it is a tree that is bearing life or one that needs to be uprooted in the name of a more inclusive theological approach that empowers women and non-binary individuals.

FBI statistics for the United States report that:

↳ 87.5% of murders are committed by men.

↳ 97.2% of forcible rapes are committed by men.

↳ 70% of violence against families and children is committed by men.[3]

Additionally, women live at higher rates of poverty than men and still do not receive equitable wages in or outside of the church. The number of women in senior leadership positions has doubled over the last decade, yet while statistics show that women leaders in the church are more likely to have a seminary education than their male counterparts, the pay gap persists in Christendom too.[4]

Even the notion of power is interpreted differently across binary gender lines. Pew Research conducted a study on language that revealed Americans are much more likely to use the word *powerful* in a positive way when it's applied to men (67% positive) and in a negative way when applied to women (92% negative).[5] In the same study, words like *provider* and *strong* were also overwhelmingly attributed to men, while words like *beautiful* or *kind* were reserved for women. Additionally, leadership and ambition were skewed to value men over women.

If we interpret these words through the lens of universalized gender roles, we might assume that men are created to be leaders and thus have culturally recognizable and innate ambition, leadership ability, and strength wired into who they are. These notions are backed up by books like John Eldridge's *Wild at Heart* that assert that a man's heart can be summarized as needing "an adventure to live, a beauty to rescue, and a battle to fight."[6] Eldridge is not unique in these assumptions that orient the heart of masculine identity toward life outside the domestic space, toward power over women, and toward violence.

The implications of this may seem simply semantic, but in situations like the 2016 Presidential race, associations with power fell on Hillary Clinton and Donald Trump differently based solely on their perceived gender identities. Clinton was seen as aggressive and was critiqued for not smiling enough, while Trump's aggressive style of speaking and interrupting was seen as a sign of powerful leadership. If that is true in politics, it is certainly true in an increasingly politicized and factious religious community. The rise of Donald Trump, particularly for the white evangelicals who are credited for putting him into office,[7] reflects a cultural comfort with and acceptance of the type of masculinity and power that Trump embodies.

Beyond Christian politics at large, the church acts out gender roles and stereotypes in ways that embolden, defend, uplift, and privilege men, giving them power over everyone who isn't a man. The semantics of many churches shed light on this phenomenon even in their subtle and possibly inadvertent usage of leadership titles. In many churches where women are not allowed in positions of leadership, women who lead ministries for women or children are called directors, while men who lead adults and children are called pastors. In some church structures, Sunday school classes for children are taught by women; but later, typically in middle and high school, the classes shift to male leadership. It is as if there is a mystical age at which boys become men and, because of their genitalia, are no longer entrusted to the leadership of women.

Simply put, the church doesn't center its politics or gender ideals around a well-thought-out theology; it gathers them from the patriarchal culture at large, slaps some proof texts on them, and systematizes the subjugation of women and the elevation of men in the name of God. It is clear that the church has adhered to a system of gender-based discrimination and exclusionary practices that have done little to develop men, and has gone to great lengths to relegate those who do not identify as men to the margins of faith communities.

That might sound harsh or unfair to you. Maybe your church has a woman pastor or otherwise encourages and supports women in leadership and seems like a great place for women to work and worship. But ask those women about their experiences of leadership, and you will find that their current positions are not an indication that arriving there has been a smooth or invitational process. They have undoubtedly had to defend their leadership against the same assumptions about their gender that I face. Until we admit the hard truth about the continued diminishment of anyone who isn't a white, cisgender male in the church, it will not change.

There is no prerequisite of bad intentions for patriarchy to persist, but the absence of bad intentions does not mean the absence of bad results. Patriarchy leads to abuse, objectification, and the exclusion of just under 50% of the human population from full participation in Jesus' kingdom work.

PATRIARCHY AND THE SEXUALIZATION OF WOMEN

When men are questioned about discipling women, it's often rooted in a long-standing church ideology that women are always sexual and, as such, are dangers to be avoided for the sake of men's piety and purity. The so-called "Billy Graham Rule," which says that men should never be alone in a space with anyone who isn't their spouse, was meant to help young men follow the call of Timothy to "flee . . . from youthful lusts" (2 Timothy 2:22, KJV). But the rule brings with it unspoken and dehumanizing assumptions about women. It assumes that women are unavoidable sexual temptations, that women provide the context for the inevitable event of men straying from their marriages. It makes women little more than objects of temptation rather than co-laborers in the gospel.

At the same time, this objectification of women dehumanizes men. It sets up an ideology in which men are simply buffoonish creatures led unknowingly or irresponsibly into sexual temptation. It robs men of the belief that they can be good leaders and good human beings, instead instilling them with stereotypical standards of what "manhood" and "womanhood" are all about. Neither gender can be fully themselves when men are forced into a box that tells them they are incapable of seeing women as people and when women are reduced to objects or sidekicks in the kingdom. This dehumanization is not the gospel; nor does it move the good news of Jesus forward.

Ironically, it is rarely women who are accused of initiating sexual misconduct or infidelity. Similarly, women are rarely sourced as the agents of a church collapse, leadership scandals, or power abuses.

In the summer of 2018, a scandal broke involving former Willow Creek pastor, Bill Hybels. In the fallout, it became clear that even (and maybe especially) in congregations with the success, reputation, and impact of Willow Creek, assumptions of men's goodness, reliability, and leadership create the context for—and defense of—abuse. Allegations of sexual misconduct were brought up against the megachurch pastor more than four years before the story gained traction with the public. While the umbrella organization ignored the accusations and Willow Creek claimed to deal with it internally, the manifestation of such "investigations" was the maligning of the abused women's character, claims that they were lying, and narratives spun about how they were putting the integrity of Willow Creek's witness at risk. There seemed to be little to no concern among the leadership that it was the abuse of power that indeed compromised the witness of the church. Until articles in which victims of this abuse told their stories came out in *The New York Times*, *Christianity Today*, and the *Chicago Tribune*, Willow Creek leadership was almost entirely unwavering in its defense of its celebrity pastor.

Churches frequently keep things that are considered issues of sin in-house, dealing with them among elder boards or within denominations instead of calling them what they are—crimes. In doing so, they protect leaders from the legal implications of their actions. Even the structures that are in place to do "justice" in faith communities disproportionately elevate the narratives of men, and gaslight and demonize victims who try to speak about their own experiences of abuse.

THE OWNERSHIP OF NON-MALE BODIES

This type of behavior and these practices are not simply a "mistake," nor can they be dismissed as the actions of a few "bad apples" in the Christian world. They are the outgrowth of a theological perspective on the role and value of women that is as pervasive as it is unbiblical. In an attempt to avoid molding to secular culture, Christians in the United States, and evangelicals in particular, have doubled down on stringent patriarchal gender roles in the name of orthodoxy without recognizing that these systems are themselves deeply embedded in secular culture. One of the primary manifestations of this syncretism is purity culture.

Purity culture was not birthed in a vacuum, but rather is the direct result of the church attempting to maintain cultural power and defend traditional family values in the name of God. It is a set of values that, while, yes, finds some support in Scripture, has greater cultural foundation than biblical. It is rooted in ancient patriarchal systems that commodified women's bodies and virginity and, through transactions like marriage, viewed women as objects with monetary value instead of humans made in the image of God.

In many ancient arranged marriages, fathers were in effect selling their daughters in exchange for property, money, and status. It was, in essence, the sale of virginity. Virginity was a cultural commodity used to bind families, generate wealth, and ensure the continuation of bloodlines. Men defended the virginity of their daughters and community members as one would defend their property, and there were strong consequences (namely death) to those who violated the solemnity of virginity. This early social construct of virginity used sexual encounters as a means of property transfer. It had almost nothing to do with virtue or protecting the marriage bond, and everything to do with guaranteeing the purity of bloodlines and full ownership of a woman by a patriarch.

Ownership of women's bodies, both ideologically and practically, allowed for the easy defense of virginity, particularly in the context of Christianity. However, by the late 1890s and early 1900s, women were beginning to assert agency over their own bodies. In the sexual revolution of the 1960s, the shift from patriarchal/kyriarchal values created a problem for the church: In the broader culture, men were no longer the arbiters of women's bodies, sexuality, and virginity. The church could no longer rely on social norms to keep women in check.

In addition, the social means of defining virginity also began to shift as heteronormative understandings of what intercourse involves were no longer sufficient to answer whether one still had their virginity. As women in greater society gained increasing autonomy, the church felt itself losing a sense of moral high ground. For evangelical institutions predominantly led by men, this also meant the potential for a massive loss of power. Men, particularly leaders in churches, perceived the rise in feminism as subverting the gospel by enticing women—over whom they previously had significant power—to reject what these men believed to be God's intention for gender.

With the loss of men's power over women in the broader culture, many Christians, particularly evangelicals, theologized purity culture and shifted the onus from virginity being about bloodlines to virginity being about one's inherent value. This is disproportionately true for women. The gendered language of virginity is telling in this context:

She gives it up . . .

She saves it for . . .

He takes it . . .

In effect, purity culture has created an idol of virginity, elevating its value over all other things about women, while largely letting men off the hook.

Underlying all of this is a set of assumptions about the so-called God-given nature of what are actually socially constructed gender identities. If we are truly interested in being "in the world but not of the world," then the faithful work of the church is to examine those assumptions through the lens of Scripture and form theology about gender that more fully resembles the way of Jesus.[8]

READING PATRIARCHY INTO THE BIBLE

To fully do justice to the biblical narrative's engagement of women and constant moves against patriarchal systems goes beyond the scope of this piece; but we can, at the least, examine significant frames that manifest an androcentric bent to our understanding of Scripture.

masculine pov center of world view

If we're going to do this work well, we need to get rid of one significant hurdle to engaging with Scripture effectively: just because a topic exists in the pages of the Bible doesn't mean it's God-ordained. Slavery was biblical because it was a cultural norm, but that doesn't mean it was God's intent. Child sacrifice exists in the pages (and not just among "those people"; don't forget

Abraham), but that doesn't make it moral. The Israelites were ethnocentric and xenophobic, but that doesn't mean we ought to be. Scripture exists and operates in ancient cultural patriarchy, but that doesn't mean that we ought to replicate it in the name of being biblical.

Every theological idea has an origin, even and especially those found in sacred texts. They don't spring out of nowhere for no reason. They speak to a time, place, and people, and are reinterpreted in other times and places by very different people who are trying to make sense of the divine. The danger is in assuming that sacred texts are devoid of interpretive bias, syncretism, or historical rootedness.

Patriarchal interpretations of Scripture tend to come at the Bible backward. They use the Old Testament as an affirmation of modern-day patriarchy without considering the ways in which the patriarchal systems of the Old Testament were upended by Jesus. These interpretations use Paul's epistles to systematically exclude women from church leadership and from equity in their marriages and relationships without recognizing the specific needs of the churches to which Paul wrote. It seems that most spaces that privilege and empower men interpret the way of Jesus through the lens of the Old Testament and/or the filter of Pauline theology, rather than having Jesus be the standard through which we understand what God has to say (or doesn't say in many cases) about women and gender-nonbinary people in the rest of the text.

As Christians, we have no choice but to make Jesus the central focus of our biblical interpretation, the filter through which everything else in Scripture in understood. If we interpret Paul and the Old Testament through the way and teachings of Jesus, we end up with a Jesus who looks more like a feminist than like the institutional misogyny of the church. Coming to Scripture backward means missing out on the ways Jesus actually interacted with and liberated women in cultures where patriarchy was the accepted social norm.

RECLAIMING GENESIS

Western elevation of the leadership of men—and, by extension, its assumptions about the inferiority, emotionality, and unreliability of women and nonbinary people—has such deep cultural roots that it becomes difficult to see where the Bible begins and cultural patriarchy ends. This is particularly evident in the core text of Genesis 1 and 2. These creation narratives have long been subject to misleading or generous interpretations that the authors likely had no intention of presenting.

In their broadest sense, these narratives are a countercultural picture of a God who, unlike other gods of the time, didn't use violence or death to create, but rather used words to make the world and everything in it. They are a series of poems meant to present the character of God and a snapshot of a creation that is regenerative by its very design. Humans enter into the story on the "sixth day;" and like the trees that produce seeds to create more trees, and the animals that pair and mate to create more animals, these humans enter into the story not only able to create more humans together, but cognitively able to name and design and categorize their surroundings, thus becoming more like their Creator.

Genesis tells a story of God creating two people in God's own image and likeness (creators that create) to *partner* together to tend to the earth. They are created without any mention of hierarchy but rather are equally tasked with tending the garden. They are to rule, or be responsible for, the world alongside God and on God's behalf. It's not until sin enters the story that any sort of hierarchical language is introduced. But in a society that is trained to elevate men on the basis of their gender alone, theologians have done textual gymnastics to defend a system of gender-based subjugation that is rooted in sin. The western church is so committed to patriarchy that it would rather sacrifice—even inadvertently—God's intentions in order to preserve the power to "rule over" others that was given to Adam after the fall.

Patriarchal theology is often rooted in this story. While the narrative is not about marriage, gender, or patriarchy specifically, our male-dominated Christian culture seems to be unable to separate the purpose of this poetry from the gender- and power-based agendas they bring to it. They take a narrative of the man being created first and the woman second to mean that man takes priority over woman and has greater purpose, rather than seeing the story of the man's loneliness as a means to create drama in the text. They take Eve being brought from Adam's rib to mean that she is to help him and forgo agency of her own, despite that same Hebrew word for helper, *ezer*, being used twenty-one times in the text to refer to God. (And frankly, Adam being made from dirt isn't the most flattering or sexy way to enter the world.) They take Eve being deceived by the serpent and claim that if the man had been "head" of his wife (a view that didn't exist until thousands of years after this text's origins) or had led his household (in a garden presumably without houses or the notion of family), the fall would never have happened. The scapegoating of women is, in this case, as old as sin.

The misinterpretation of the creation accounts also arises from a conflation of the first and second poems. One poem refers to sex—male and female—and the other refers to gender—man and woman. In the first poem the text says:

> "So God created humankind in his image,
>   in the image of God he created them;
>   male and female he created them" (Genesis 1:27).

God creates the proto-humans equally in the image of God and, while creating two sexes, doesn't claim that the creative force of God ends there. The creation narrative is the start of a generative story, not a "one-and-done" universal account of all that God intends to create or that will exist. Historically, the church has conflated sex and gender and used this poem to erase, demonize, and exclude those who exist outside of cisgender, heteronormative expressions of gender and sexuality. It's important that we not limit modern reality to a narrow interpretation of sex based in an ancient text.

The creation narratives largely have been used as a static standard to enforce societal gender roles, even though the narratives emphasize partnership and creative capacity, not marriage (which was completely different then than our understanding of it today), gender roles (that didn't exist), or church leadership (which it says nothing about and has nothing to do with). The universalizing of marriage and gender ideals from these poems is a diversion from the point of the text. It is losing the forest for the most masculine-presenting and patriarchy-enforcing trees.

The patriarchal assumptions that spring from the creation narrative gave rise to the bastardized interpretation of the cultural norms in ancient Israel and every story about women in the Bible. It shaped the way readers engage with leaders and heroes like Deborah, Jael, Esther, and Ruth in the Old Testament. And it affects how we interpret Jesus' interactions with women.

JESUS THE EGALITARIAN

The conceptual frameworks of patriarchy were alive and well in Jesus' day, so much so that much of his engagement with people and with power can best be understood by noticing the ways in which he subverts those frameworks. Jesus seems almost entirely disinterested in power in the conventional sense. He doesn't rely on violence, domination, fear-mongering, arguing, or "mansplaining" faith to the women he encounters. Instead, the triune God invites a woman to grow Jesus' body and give birth to him. (I'm sure God could have picked plenty of ways to show up, but chose to be carried by a woman.) Jesus invites women to be his disciples and to learn, to take a central role in his parables, to defend him, to interrupt the problematic sexual-religious culture that blamed and demonized them, to fund his ministry and walk with him, and to be the first witnesses of and evangelists about his resurrected body. After his ascension, women became leaders of house churches, served as prophets and apostles in the early church, and were revered for their leadership and contributions to the faith.

I wonder how many of those things could be said of the church today.

While Jesus sat with the shamed and judged Samaritan woman, the church uses purity culture to reduce women's value to their sexuality.

While Jesus invited women to be witnesses of the resurrection and to tell the men about it, the church silences women in the name of headship and propriety.

While Jesus invited women to be his disciples and sit at *his* feet, the church invites women to sit at the feet of men in order to be taught the way of Jesus.

The church in the United States looks more like a disciple of patriarchal culture than a disciple of the way of Jesus. It has taken the way of power, control, domination, and entitlement, and confused it for the self-sacrificing, inclusive, chaotic, unpredictable, and downwardly mobile way of Jesus. It has claimed moral authority through oppressive practices and flaccid proof texts that elevate men at the expense of others, allowing one group of people to control most religious spaces and become the arbiters of what is right, holy, and orthodox.

In contrast, Jesus doesn't relegate women and nonbinary people to subservient roles. He doesn't belittle them. He doesn't dictate which spaces they can influence. He doesn't police their clothing or appearance. He doesn't silence them. Jesus hung out with prostitutes, mothers, housewives, those with money and certainly those without, those with demons, those with reputations, those with sexual histories, and those who were hated. Jesus wasn't just *for* them, but actually *with* them. He seemed to see them as co-laborers in the kingdom he was building.

If patriarchy were God's dream for the world, Jesus sure didn't try very hard to make it happen.

Jesus tells us to pick up our cross daily, to die to ourselves, to give our lives for others. There is loss in choosing the way of the kingdom. For men, this might mean it's time to lay aside the life of privilege that their gender or sex gives them and sacrifice the entitlement to and need for power. It might mean handing over the reins of power in churches, confronting other men on their violence toward and sexualization of women, and losing members who worship at the altar of male privilege. It might mean shining a light on all the ways in which people who aren't white, cisgender, straight men have been pushed to the margins, where they are abused, silenced, and made to feel invisible. It might mean putting an end to justifying, protecting, and excusing the harm done to folks who reside there.

At the end of the day, patriarchy hurts us all. It disempowers men from expressing weakness, fear, tenderness, and other so-called feminine feelings. It devalues those who don't lead through domination. It makes women into sexual objects—excluded helpers, subservient partners, and silenced co-laborers. It dehumanizes those who are outside the power structures of political, social, and religious life in our country.

And that doesn't look anything like Jesus.

Brandi Miller is on staff with Intervarsity Christian Fellowship and spends her time musing on the role of practical theology in racial justice. When she isn't working, you can find her critiquing bougie coffee, listening to Justin Bieber, or in the gym Olympic weightlifting. You can follow her endeavors at stirringupholymischief.com or on twitter at @brandinico.

ENDNOTES

1   rupi kaur, *Milk and Honey,* (Kansas City, KS: Andrews Mc-
     Meel Publishing, 2015), 45.

2   "Religious Landscape Study, Gender Composition," Pew
     Research Forum, 2014, accessed October 2, 2018. http://www.
     pewforum.org/religious-landscape-study/gender-composi-
     tion/.

3   "Crime in the United States, 2017," Federal Bureau of Investi-
     gation: Uniform Crime Reporting Program, accessed October
     2, 2018, https://ucr.fbi.gov/crime-in-the-u.s/2017/crime-in-
     the-u.s.-2017/tables/table-42.

4   "Gender Pay Gap Among Clergy Worse than National Av-
     erage," Religion News Service, accessed October 2, 2018,
     https://religionnews.com/2016/01/12/gender-pay-gap-among-
     clergy-worse-than-national-average-a-first-look-at-the-new-na-
     tional-data/.

5   Kristi Walker, Kristen Bialik, and Patricia van Kessel,
     "Strong Men, Caring Women," Pew Social Trends, July 24,
     2018, http://www.pewsocialtrends.org/interactives/strong-
     men-caring-women/.

6   John Eldredge, "Real Men: Your Core Passions," Ransomed
     Heart, accessed October 2, 2018, http://www.ransomedheart.
     com/story/real-men/your-core-passions.

7   "How the faithful voted: A preliminary 2016 analysis," Pew
     Research Center, accessed October 2, 2018, http://www.
     pewresearch.org/fact-tank/2016/11/09/how-the-faithful-vot-
     ed-a-preliminary-2016-analysis/.

8   It is notable in these conversations that there has been
     little room afforded people who do not identify in the gender
     binary. While Scripture does not ignore the existence of
     people outside the binary (see, for example, the story of Jacob
     and Esau, where Jacob is identified in terms that set his
     more feminine gendering in opposition to his brother's more
     masculine gendering; or Deborah, who defied gender norms
     as a judge; or the relationship between David and Jonathan
     that suggests—at the very least—a level of love and care for
     one another that is unusual enough to warrant mention in
     the biblical narrative), the mainstream church, in its historic
     homophobia and heteronormativity, has all but erased nonbi-
     nary people from the theological (missiological and ecclesio-
     logical) conversation.

2

I KISSED NICENESS GOODBYE

HOW WOMEN CAN OVERCOME SHAME AND RECLAIM OURSELVES

BY CARLA EWERT AND LINDA KAY KLEIN

Women's sexuality has long been a topic of discussion in the church, from the perpetuation of the Madonna/Whore myth that suggests women are limited to two versions of sexual expression—all or none, to debates about women's bodies and contraception, to wrestling with the emergence of the #MeToo and #ChurchToo movements. We, Linda and Carla, grew up in the white, American evangelical church of the 1980s and '90s largely surrounded by conservative perspectives on these conversations. Carla was a pastor's daughter; Linda planned to become a missionary. However, as we grew into women, we found ourselves questioning some of what we learned about gender and sexuality in the church. We found some teachings to be insufficient and others to be downright debilitating.

While our experience is grounded in our specific religious upbringing, the professional work each of us has done exploring gender and sexuality has shown us that much of what we were taught in our evangelical churches is not taught only here; and that these teachings affect the lives of a wide range of men, women and people of all backgrounds. What follows is an overview of how some of what we were taught came about, and the ways in which these teachings inform and shape many women's understandings of our personhood and our relationships with others, including God.

Linda:

I spent twelve years documenting stories of sexual shame from women raised in the white, American evangelical Christian church for my book, *Pure: Inside the Evangelical Movement That Shamed a Generation of Young Women and How I Broke Free.* Yet there was one trend among my interviewees' stories that I didn't write about in the book. I'd like to tell you about it here through the story of my friend Katie, who grew up in the same church as I.

One evening, Katie and I were having dinner. She was telling me about a female co-worker who deeply impressed her: "She would just say, 'And now I need to go to the bathroom.'" Katie mimicked the woman's matter-of-fact tone with a grin. "Or 'I need it to be quiet right now.' Or 'Thank you for inviting me to lunch, but I really need to know these things in advance.'"

Katie grabbed her napkin off her lap and wiped at the edges of her mouth, laughing. "Me? I'm just the suck-it-up girl. Even if I'm uncomfortable with a social situation, or I'm not really in a good place, I go. I go because the other person wants it and it'll make them happy. It's hard for me to say, 'No, I'm not in the mood,' or 'No, I'm tired,' or 'It's been a hard day at work'—all valid reasons not to do things. But for some reason, they don't feel valid for me."

"Then, a couple of months ago, I had this thought," Katie said, her face brightening. "I was like, 'I'm a *person* actually. Those things are as real for me as they are for other people.'" Katie leaned over the table toward me and looked me dead in the eye, as though telling me something utterly revelatory.

"I'm a *person*," she repeated.

One of the most surprising things to come up in my interviews was the frequency with which women told me they didn't feel like "a person." In time, I started to pay attention to when they used the phrase and why. I realized that in every instance, they were referring to times of their lives in which some inner truth—their feelings, their beliefs, their experiences, their desires, or their identity—was denied.

Sometimes this truth was denied by someone else.

More often it was denied by the woman herself.

These women were so aware of the expectations of who they were supposed to be that they wound up ignoring—and sometimes even losing touch with— who they *were*. Some hid parts of themselves or their lives; some kept trauma locked deep inside of them, acting as though they were fine when, really, they were anything but; some simply did what they knew others wanted them to do without ever asking what they wanted themselves. They felt like other people were permitted the full range of desire, emotion, and experience—others could be selfish, scared, messed up, needy— you know, human—but not them. In other words, the women had internalized inhuman expectations for themselves, and that made them feel inhuman.

This made me wonder: What causes some of us women to deny our inner truth, and why does it have such a dehumanizing effect on us when we do it?

Carla:

While Linda was interviewing women around the country, I was turning toward a more progressive form of Christianity, having recently abandoned the conservative evangelical church I was raised in. I'd grown tired of gender expectations that limited my involvement and had ended up nose deep in Renaissance literature, working on a master's degree. As I studied characters like Britomart, Desdemona, and Eve crafted by writers like Edmund Spenser, William Shakespeare, and John Milton, I was struck by a recurring pattern in their stories.

Each of the characters I studied is required to mistrust her inner voice to pay attention to an external voice, often a male one; to separate herself from her own experience and see herself as part of a man's experience instead. *Each is cut off from her own direct purpose by external influences of power, such as religious and cultural norms and external expectations. Each expresses profound unease in her experience.

For example, in John Milton's *Paradise Lost,* Eve comments on the gendered arrangement in the garden when she addresses Adam as "thou for whom / And from whom I was formed . . . / And without whom am to no end."[1] Adam is the fulcrum on which Eve pivots, and without him, she is unhinged and "to no end." Eve's words expose a feeling of purposelessness and even despair over her place in this patriarchal system of value and worth. *These words well written by a man*

Milton's presentation of Adam and Eve reflects a commonly held doctrine of the early modern church: Men were made in the image of God while women were made in the image of men. Women, then, only experienced the full image and presence of God when joined with a man. It followed that men had access to divine voice and inspiration, while women were cut off from divinity. This distance between women and the divine has been used to craft a patriarchal theology that portrays God as male and women as spiritually inferior. As a result, women are denied individual freedom—all women are like Eve, existing for the sake of someone else. Women are *to be experienced* rather than *to experience.* This is the existential disappointment that the women Linda interviewed described when they said they didn't feel like a person.

Linda and I met when we were each presenting our research at a conference. Imagine our surprise when we compared notes and saw that the same patterns that showed up in her interviews

* growing up I wanted to be a secretary to a man rising in a corp (subservient) and rise with him (power through him)

were right there in the female characters I studied in some of the most prominent literature of the early modern period. That this sixteenth- and seventeenth-century pattern extends to the experience of twenty-first-century women strongly suggests that the doctrines of that early modern period are not only alive and well in today's patriarchal systems; they are pervasive and insidious.

Linda and I wrote the following in an attempt to make sense of the ways in which these teachings often inform and shape a woman's understanding of our personhood and our relationships with others, including God.

A THEOLOGY OF NICENESS

Though all Christians are taught to subvert their own wants and needs at times, honoring the wants and needs of others, whether this teaching plays out more positively or negatively in people's lives can be greatly influenced by gender expectations. It's very healthy for someone who is taught by society to prioritize themselves and their own success—as men often are—to be encouraged to prioritize other people. The teaching becomes a balancing tool. However, when one is taught by society to consistently prioritize others over themselves—as women often are—this same teaching can lead to further *imbalance in the* individual's life, leading some women to de-prioritize themselves to an unhealthy and potentially dangerous extent.

Most women have experienced some version of being told that a "good" woman puts others first, ensuring that her husband, children, friends, and family members are comfortable, happy, and cared for before she tends to herself. However, women raised in *complementarian* churches, like the two of us were, may be nodding their heads more fervently than others while reading this.

Complementarianism teaches that all people, men and women, are created in God's image (this is an improvement on the early modern doctrine discussed above). Yet men are created to be leaders. Their God-given nature suits them to be in positions of power. Women, meanwhile, are created to be helpers. Their God-given nature suits them to be in positions of service. The genders "complement" each other in these differences—hence the name. We have particular roles, and regardless of our giftedness or desires, we are obligated first to the expectations of our gender.

Of course, complementarianism is really just one of the most recent expressions of the longstanding patriarchal system that has been baked into so much of the modern Christian church and is laced throughout society as a whole.

A brief refresher on patriarchy might be helpful here. Patriarchy reflects a theology that believed in a stratified universe with God at the top as the separate, supreme being. Patriarchy, likewise, is a stratified humanity with male at the top of the hierarchy and, therefore, closest to God (you can see where John Milton got his ideas). This ideology is imposed retroactively on the creation stories in Genesis, creating grounds for religious systems to claim it as the "natural" order and a reason to maintain what has proven to be an oppressive power structure.

Patriarchy maintains its power in part by acting as if it's based on a biblical or biological imperative—that it's just the way things are. It further maintains power through the invisibility that results from that teaching—if we can't see it, if we assume it's natural, we won't believe we can change it. But when we can recognize that something is a social construct that we can choose to participate in or not, we can see it for what it is and decide whether or not we want it to change.

Patriarchal teachings create conditions that dehumanize and subjugate all people (think of how we tell boys to "man up" in the face of challenges rather than admit fear or weakness), but women bear a particular burden. We are expected to follow the rules of our gender *and* do so in a way that's helpful and pleasing to men. This leaves women twice removed from our internal voice—once by the norms of our own gender and again by the way our gender sits in service to men. Again, the words of Eve to Adam in *Paradise Lost* articulate the assumption: "Both have sinned, but thou / Against God only, I against God and thee."[2]

We might call this double removal the "Theology of Niceness." The Theology of Niceness doesn't tell women what to *do*—treat people kindly, or love others, or fight for justice for the oppressed. Rather, it tells us what *not* to do. We learn that "nice" girls and women:

> *don't* upset people by saying things they don't want to hear;

> *don't* make people uncomfortable by showing "ugly" emotions;

> *don't* disappoint people or hurt people's feelings;

> *don't* talk about upsetting topics;

> *don't* spend too much time pursuing their own happiness when they could be pursuing the happiness of others;

> in short, *don't* do anything to upset anyone or make any person (especially men) uncomfortable . . . ever.

Women who master the Theology of Niceness learn to be passive and pliable, prepared at any moment to meet the needs of others. By focusing so much on others, they can begin to feel distant from themselves—less sure of what *they* want, what *they* need, what *they* believe, even of what they *feel*. Other people become the subjects of their lives—their husbands, their children, their friends, their parents—while they are left to fit themselves into the blank spaces around those subjects, taking up only as much space as is left for them, their shape defined by the shapes of others. Whatever humanity we women have inside ourselves is to be subverted so that we can be good wives, good mothers, good friends, and good Christians.

So, what does any of this have to do with sexuality? Well, let us introduce you to purity culture. If patriarchal teachings like complementarianism have created the pressure for women to shape themselves to male expectations, purity culture extends this teaching to the sexual sphere.

PURELY PURITY

While the basic tenet of purity culture is that any sex act outside of heterosexual marriage is wrong, purity culture further teaches that sexual feelings and thoughts should be suppressed—especially if you're a woman or a girl. A woman's so-called "purity" is said to be the greatest gift she can give her future husband, making some women feel reduced to their bodies and their service to others.

Purity culture also teaches that sexual desire is a primarily male experience and that many men simply "can't help themselves" when a woman "leads" them into lust. Women, who are said to be less sexual, are therefore held responsible for their own desires as well as those of men. They must dress modestly so as not to make their brothers in Christ "stumble." Before marriage, women are expected to guard their sexual purity and wait patiently until they are guided to the right partner. As author Jessica Valenti writes in her book *The Purity Myth*:

> Staying "pure" and "innocent" is touted as the greatest thing we can do. However, equating this inaction with morality is not only problematic because it continues to tie women's ethics to our bodies, but also is downright insulting because it suggests that women can't be moral actors. Instead, we're defined by what we don't do—our ethics are the ethics of passivity.[3]

Growing up in the evangelical church, the two of us both read a lot of Christian books about sex and dating. We both remember noticing the difference in the ways that girls/women and boys/men were being talked to and taught about sex and sexuality in these books. The titles of the books written for boys and men were active, inspiring their readers to go out and fight—and win! For example, the best-selling Every Man's Battle series includes *Every Man's Battle: Every Man's Guide to Winning the War on Sexual Temptation One Victory at a Time* and *Every Young Man's Battle: Strategies for Victory in the Real World of Sexual Temptation.* The titles of the books written for girls and women, meanwhile, encouraged the kind of passivity Valenti describes. Consider the companion Every Woman's Battle series: *Every Woman's Battle: Discovering God's Plan for Sexual and Emotional Fulfillment* and *Every Young Woman's Battle: Guarding Your Mind, Heart, and Body in a Sex-Saturated World.*

After marriage, however, purity culture's message for women takes a big turn. After years of shutting off our sexual desire (because women do have sexual desire), we are instantly expected to transform into our partner's red-hot sexual satisfier, ensuring he will never leave or cheat on us.

Making this transition can be difficult—and sometimes impossible. Some women get so good at shutting their sexual feelings off that they find it difficult to turn them on later. Even women who might have been sexually active before marriage can hold on to so much inherited shame for coming into a marriage without their virginity intact that they can't allow themselves to enjoy sex. Others, meanwhile, are able to be sexual but struggle to name just what it is, *exactly*, that they want sexually, having only ever been asked what others want *of* them, resulting in a less satisfying sexual life than they'd like. And even when women do know themselves well, they may still find themselves doing things they don't want to do and feeling confused and alone after a sexual experience.

For many women, the #MeToo movement has brought up memories of sexual experiences they knew they didn't want but didn't realize they could say no to. In other words, cutting women off from their "yes" can also cut them off from their "no" and make abuse difficult to name. We may find ourselves in situations we know in our gut we need to get out of, only to have our training in the Theology of

Niceness kick in, telling us we're probably just being paranoid and shouldn't upset the other person. Many women are more paralyzed by fear of not being seen as "nice" or "good" than fear of violence. And sometimes we're right. Because many men have been trained, in many cases, to expect the acquiescence of women, women can be in danger if they are direct and don't couch a rejection in niceness. But of course, being nice can also put women in danger, keeping us in dangerous situations even when everything in us says, "Run!"

These enforced gender imbalances and sexual shaming aren't just damaging to women. These messages reduce all people to being defined by their sexuality and sexual desires, a truly dehumanizing experience.

THE ROOTS OF REPRESSION

When the wellbeing of others is seen as more important than and/ or in competition with our own wellbeing—their thoughts more important than our thoughts, their feelings more important than our feelings, their needs more important than ours and so on—not only can we be hurt, but our relationships with others can be hurt. We cannot connect fully with others, bringing honesty and intimacy, if we are not even able to access and value the most honest, intimate parts of ourselves.

While we've focused primarily on the dehumanization of women, all genders have the experience of being separated from themselves through external expectations. If we have been told that our thoughts and feelings are not only less important than the thoughts and feelings of others; but also that God disapproves of our deepest impulses, we are steeped in shame and it can be difficult to reclaim our internal voices.

Growing up, the two of us often heard God portrayed as a judge and ruler who can dictate and punish. Having been raised with doctrines like total depravity and original sin, Carla was convinced she was bad, deserving condemnation. These doctrines tell us that our inner voice can't be trusted, that our will is opposed to God's will and that the only reason to know ourselves is so we know which needs and desires to sacrifice. This circular argument works like this: You make the wrong choices when you listen to your inner voice and not God's voice; you can never make the right choice because you are inherently sinful; so if you listen to your own desire, you will always be out of God's will and God will always be judging you.

Carla remembers trying to work against her own guiding voice, listening for it so she would know what not to do, then trying to determine what to do based on external opinions or teaching. She found herself wondering if she was saying and doing the right things. She understood God's will as a particular set of preordained choices that she had to discern, or be condemned to unhappiness. Unhappiness always indicated a lack of discernment or a misstep that implied she hadn't sacrificed fully or listened closely enough.

Since she had been taught to mistrust her desires rather than align with them, dissatisfaction was an almost inevitable result, and she was left disoriented in her relationships with herself, others, and God.

Remember Katie above? Her desire to please others and her desire to please God followed a similar pattern of subverting her own needs to make someone else happy, ultimately damaging her relationship with God for a time. Linda records more of Katie's story in her book, where Katie says:

> I just felt no guidance from God, and I started taking it personally after a while. I didn't feel like God kept his end of the bargain in terms of leading me and guiding me. I always thought that he had a plan and purpose for us and I was like, why wouldn't he tell me what that was, or at least let me feel what that was, or somehow shut the doors in some way so I have to go this other direction. I felt abandoned. I tried talking to him. Why wouldn't he talk to me? I just felt silence from Heaven. That was the first time I started walking away from

God a little bit in my heart. . . . I was just so mad at God. I was really upset and disappointed. I wasn't finding an evangelical man or a meaningful career—all the things that I wanted. So I was feeling frustrated. I had four or five avenues that I thought about as a vocation for myself, but I was just really looking for guidance from God: "Where would you want me to be, God?" It's funny because it really never occurred to me that maybe he was letting me choose. It never even occurred to me that he would be saying, "And here's your life; do what you want."[4]

For those of us raised in churches where we were taught that even God is not interested in our authentic selves, finding our way through the shame, the judgment, and the belief that our very essence is flawed can take a lifetime of work.

RETURNING TO OUR HUMANITY

To connect with ourselves and others, we have to reassess our relationship to our inner voice. This doesn't mean we should be irresponsible and selfish, always putting ourselves and our own wants and needs above those of other people. It *does* mean we should know ourselves and be capable of making conscious, informed choices about when to prioritize ourselves and when to prioritize others—rather than putting others first as a constant, knee-jerk reaction.

Linda has noticed another trend in her research, one that can guide our thinking as we figure out how to overcome these damaging messages of subversion. As often as the women Linda interviewed described not feeling like a person, they also described *feeling* like one. Linda noticed that they felt like a person when referring to periods of their lives in which their true feelings, thoughts, desires, beliefs, and experiences were honored. Being honored—by themselves and by others—was *re*-humanizing.

Take Meagan. She described a period of her life in which she lived solely for others, denying even a deeply felt calling to become a pastor because other people thought women shouldn't be pastors. "I just wasn't a person," she told Linda. "I had no self. So much of myself was underground. I was just like, 'This is the thing that you're supposed to do. This is the good thing. And I'm good, so I'm doing it.'"

Eventually, Meagan came to know, acknowledge, and honor the voice inside her that one might call the Holy Spirit. Today, Meagan is a pastor. She loves serving her church and feels like her authentic self in the role. But every once in a while, Meagan admitted, she hears the voices of those in her childhood complementarian Christian church who told her women can't preach. She said that in those moments, "I feel like I'm not a person. I'm back in that place." Even though Meagan now knows she's a whole person, she also knows there are many who would rather she sit down and be a "nice" girl again.

We can also find inspiration in the stories of women in the Bible. Look no further than our foremother Mary, a fierce soul. The sister of Martha and Lazarus, Mary seems to always do the wrong thing at the wrong time. She sits at Jesus' feet in the posture of a student—at the time, a position only allowed to men and boys. She lets her curiosity and desire pull her into interaction with God.

She does this again—acts on pure wanting and passion—just before Jesus' death. A version of this story is told in every Gospel, but the woman is only clearly identified in John 12:1-8. Matthew and Mark tell it as an anointing of Jesus' head, which Rachel Held Evans points out echoes the tradition of priests anointing kings, suggesting that the writers are aligning the woman in these passages with a priest and prophet.[5] In Luke, the woman is called a sinner and the disciples are shocked that Jesus would welcome her passion and let her touch him.

But in John, the woman is identified as Mary, who has regularly acted on her longing to be near Jesus, who has rejected the identity imposed on her by society in order to act from a place of true agency—agency that is connected to her deepest desire. In this story, she breaks an alabaster bottle of perfume that's worth a year's wages. She lets down her hair, which in her culture was considered an erotic move. She pours the oil on Jesus' feet and then wipes them with her hair. There is no way to read this, to picture it, and deny the passion of this moment.

Mary felt the deepest calling of her heart and acted on it. There were so many reasons for her not to, so many imposed expectations of her identity to let go of in order for her to get to the point of action.

Jesus could have held up his identity as a man as a shield. He could have rebuked her, as his disciples did, for her extravagance or her lack of control. To do so would have been to protect all things about manhood and Godhood that his followers wanted him to protect. He could have held tight to his identity as a man and held her to her identity as a woman. But he didn't, and Mary knew he wouldn't. He had welcomed her before. He had acted outside of his prescribed identity, and she knew she was safe to do the same.

Not only did Jesus welcome her passion; he honored it as an act of understanding and care. More than that, in the next chapter Jesus echoes her act. Her behavior informs his when he washes his disciples' feet. His expression of love and care is built out of hers. The disciples couldn't have helped but remember the passion of Mary when Jesus knelt to wash their feet.

This is a beautiful expression of community—to see the deep humanity of one another and to allow ourselves to take part in relationships from our own deep places of personhood. What if we listened to and shared our deepest internal voices boldly and kindly—what could we learn from one other? Imagine how we could be shaped by our real experiences of one another and our real experiences of community, were we to replace the gendered theology of niceness with a theology of connection.

When we practice showing up and allowing ourselves to be touched by our interactions with each other, the world, and God, we experience connection. We feel and follow our curiosity and, in doing so, make space for others to do the same. We stop manipulating relationships by crafting a pleasing identity for others to respond to and, instead, show up with vulnerability and allow ourselves to feel and respond in relationships. This is our living offering—to bring what we actually are and offer it in relationship—a theology of connection that allows us to live as full persons with each other and in God.

Linda Kay Klein is the author of Pure: Inside the Evangelical Movement that Shamed a Generation of Young Women and How I Broke Free *(Touchstone, 2018), and the founder of Break Free Together, an organization that helps people to release shame and claim their whole selves.*

Carla Ewert is a Minneapolis-based writer and speaker. She is the host of Holy Writ Podcast, *a regular panelist on the* Christian Feminist Podcast, *and co-creator and director of the national conversation for women in leadership,* She Is Called.

ENDNOTES

1   John Milton, *Paradise Lost: A Norton Critical Edition.* Ed. Scott Elledge. (New York: Norton, 1993), 4.440–42.

2   Ibid. 10.930–31.

3   Jessica Valenti, *The Purity Myth: How America's Obsession with Virginity Is Hurting Young Women* (Berkeley, CA: Seal Press, 2009), 24–25.

4   Linda Kay Klein, *Pure: Inside the Evangelical Movement That Shamed a Generation of Young Women and How I Broke Free* (New York: Touchstone, 2018), 130–131.

5   Rachel Held Evans, "Women of the Passion Anoint Oil," Rachel Held Evans, accessed Sept. 24, 2018, https://rachelheldevans.com/blog/women-of-the-passion-anoint-oil/.

3

SEX AND MARRIAGE

THE SEARCH FOR HOLY INTIMACY

DR. TINA SCHERMER SELLERS

I opened my email and saw the subject line: "Help! I thought I did it right, but it's gone to hell!" I'd been traveling and speaking about ancient Hebrew sources of erotic wisdom and had a backlog of messages. But this one from a woman named Stacey jumped out at me.

Stacey wrote:

> I heard you speak recently at a women's conference. Your words resonated deeply with me—they stirred up old pain, but gave me new hope at the same time. I knew that what I'd been told about sex in my growing-up years was counterfeit, but your naming it has helped me believe my own knowing. I grew up focusing on everyone else, believing that if I took care of others and tried to be kind and good, everything would work out. I married Tyler, the nice Christian boy, when I was very young— but before long, I found myself accommodating him in every

way imaginable. Our sex life was all about making him feel good. I never thought about me. Sex was on his time, when he wanted it, how he wanted it. We were to a point where I would try to make him think that everything he was doing to me was making me feel good, just so he could feel good about himself. He didn't seem able to handle criticism or instruction.

Stacey went on to explain that about eight years into their marriage, she began to speak up more frequently to Tyler, trying to make space for her own opinions and desires. She quickly learned, however, that Tyler couldn't handle it without becoming defensive and withdrawing into depression. She wrote:

> I'd revert into caretaking and try to bolster him. I needed his help running our family, and I couldn't afford for him to disappear physically and emotionally. But as I acquiesced into silence and accommodation, I would start to feel more and more empty inside, like I was becoming invisible even to myself, and I would eventually start to speak up again. Tyler and I were in a vicious cycle: I'd feel powerless, I'd speak out, Tyler would disappear into himself, I'd cave and try to shore up his emotions, so I'd feel trapped again, so I'd speak up—and around and around we'd go. The more times we went around that circle, the more unhappy I became, and our marriage slowly unraveled. We divorced just shy of our twelve-year anniversary. That was two years ago.

DIS-INTEGRATION AND THE BIRTH OF SHAME

Stacey's message pointed to something that countless others have experienced: the denial of our sexuality because we've been trained to separate our bodies from our being. Long before Jesus arrived on the scene, Aristotle and Plato cemented what has become known as the mind/body split, or mind/body dualism. They argued that the mind and the body, two different substances, occupied a hierarchical relationship in which the mind was the greater element and the body more of a burden. This dualism has caused countless personal, relational, and theological problems for thousands of years, especially for women.

Because the experiences of birth and nurturing are intensely physical, it was assumed that women were mostly of the body and had less access to the mind and spirit. It followed, then, that women were only fully spiritual when connected with a man, who was of the mind. This was the beginning of the hierarchical arrangement we know today as patriarchy. It gave a framework by which men were thought of as the head over the baser, bodily women. And being bound to the body also meant that women were sources of men's sexual temptation. Therefore, women were seen as something to be controlled and resisted—mind over body. When men failed to live up to standards of sexual conduct, they blamed women as the cause.

This dis-integration of the human experience set the stage for the fourth-century Christian church, under Constantine's rule, to develop a distinctly sex-negative, woman-negative sexual ethic. Men, vying for position and power in the young church, demonstrated their spiritual prowess by denying the body and its natural desires for connection and pleasure, elevating the spiritual mind as master over the base body. It's important to understand that the "skill" of rejecting physical connection and pleasure had nothing to do with the life, death, and resurrection of Jesus. It was based on the dis-integration of the human person—on severing the inherent oneness of mind and body, thereby disavowing a major part of the human experience.

Having aligned women with the physical, the church and culture paved the way for women to be reduced to sexual objects, all while the God-given human desire for connection and pleasure came to be seen by most people in authority as perverted and something to be conquered. Naturally, women became the holding space for that projected shame. Fast-forward a couple thousand years and we see the ways this patriarchal structure has evolved into the sexual and relational norms that permeate our culture, including American Christianity.

When the church began to deny physical connection and pleasure as a birthright of God's creation, it was the genesis of what would eventually become a system of deep interpersonal and sexual shame, a development that damaged the church's ability to absorb and reflect the love of God. Shame is the belief that one is unworthy of love and acceptance. In the church, that belief, when applied to sexual desire, created the conditions for people to feel unworthy of God's love and acceptance. By adopting a dualist view of the human person, the church led people to believe that they weren't God's beloved. In many cases, experiencing any form of sexual desire was seen as an example of human fallenness, something to be avoided whenever possible. Shame and pleasure—sexual pleasure in particular—became inextricably bound.

Shame is incredibly toxic on its own, but when it's connected to sexuality, sexual expression, and sexual desire, it can manifest as a sense of humiliation and disgust toward one's own body, and a belief in oneself as abnormal, inferior, and unworthy. It can teach people to suspect each other (shame toward the human body implies that one's partner is unworthy too), which dampens trust, communication, and intimacy. And shame runs deep. In Christian circles, shame and sex are so tied together that we often don't recognize the connection and pass the shame/sex dynamic down through generation after generation.

In my work as a therapist, I see the ways shame can develop across the lifespan, often beginning before a child can speak. For example, when toddlers excitedly share the pleasure-discovery of their penis or clitoris with someone, parents often rebuke them for doing so. Childhood experiences like this can settle in and fester in a child's memory over time, perhaps developing into an internal voice of self-criticism, undermining self-confidence in one's goodness or the goodness of those around them. And that leads to letters like the one I got from Stacey.

THE DESIRE DISCONNECT

Stacey's email highlights the effect of the mind/body split on the ways many Christians couples navigate sexuality within their marriage. I find that so many women enter marriage without a basic understanding of female sexual pleasure. If they've been taught anything at all, it typically centers on reproduction (periods and babies) and how men experience pleasure. Women often aren't aware that they can experience pleasure in sex or that they deserve to expect it for themselves. If they do venture into exploring pleasure on their own, there's usually someone nearby—a friend, a relative, a pastor giving a sermon—ready to call them a slut or worse. That leads women to hide their desires, especially from their male partners, afraid that the men will somehow feel threatened. In short, as unwitting heirs to the mind/body split, many women are drowning in sexual shame, immersed in centuries of misplaced patriarchal blame, afraid to feel the delicious power that lies just beneath the surface of their desires.

Interestingly, a big exception to that pattern can be found in same-sex relationships, for several reasons. For starters, same-sex relationships tend, as a rule, to feature people more or less evenly matched in their sexual development. I find that lesbian women tend to choose female partners who understand or misunderstand female sexuality to roughly the same degree as they do themselves, and men tend to understand or misunderstand equally as well. Given that lesbian and gay couples enter their relationships already willing to resist a structure that has told them for thousands of years how their sexual relationships ought to look, many feel a certain freedom to craft a sexual relationship the way they want, dispelling myths together, exploring and learning together, and sharing a remarkable sense of liberation. They often come into their relationships with a willingness to learn and to be creative.

Some heterosexual couples show an aptitude for thinking creatively too, in spite of the sexual shame that has permeated our culture both inside and outside of the church. But those couples are the exception, not the rule. From Stacey's email, it was clear to me that she and Tyler had enacted the same patterns most heterosexual couples do, and that they had tacitly colluded to focus on his pleasure early on, at the expense of hers. Neither of them had been given comprehensive sex education in their formative years or even as adults, and so they were both missing a solid understanding of how male and female anatomy and pleasure are similar and different. So many men I work with feel duped when they get married and find that their wives are not interested in sex, or at least not the kind of sex that they (the men) want to have. Many husbands bring a male-centric, intercourse-focused understanding of sexuality with them into marriage and what they hope their wives will give them. When the reality turns out to be something other than that, both partners are confused and frustrated.

Tyler, for example, hadn't been taught that the female arousal cycle is much slower than a male's, and that the vast majority of females have responsive desire (they feel desire for sex after a stimulus begins to turn them on) rather than spontaneous desire, like men usually have (sexual desire that comes on without a stimulus). For a heterosexual couple, the fact that these differences are real requires not only that men and women obtain relevant sexual knowledge in order to understand the dynamics at work between them, but also that both partners commit to the negotiation, consent-giving, and communication skills they need in order to thrive together.

Pop culture and its nonstop messages about sex leave both men and women feeling uncertain of what they are supposed to want or how they are supposed to behave in a sexual relationship. Popular images of masculinity promote the idea that a real man knows how to please his partner. Asking their mates about touch or sexual preferences threatens to reveal perceived weaknesses in their capacity as lovers—and as men.

Women don't have it any better, because if they show any interest in exploring their bodies or learning their sexual preferences before marriage, they're labeled as whores. Furthermore, the popular understanding of male-female sexuality and desire bears little resemblance to the complexity of how men and women actually think and feel, and how they experience the world.

Women are experts at nuance and beauty, and when they feel permission to care for themselves the way they care for others, they can be incredibly creative with how they bring pleasure to themselves and to those around them, including their sexual partners. As long as there is no goal for anything else—if sex isn't just about male orgasm, and if it focuses solely on mutual pleasure and intimacy—many women are all too happy to explore their own eroticism in fresh ways. A woman might meet her partner in a warm bath, with champagne, candles, and music, or perhaps something even a bit more daring. She can take the lead and come up with all kinds of ideas that are so much more interesting and satisfying to her than the typical masculine menu of a little fondling followed by three minutes of intercourse. If there's no kind of orgasmic "end" in mind, if the woman can bring all of her giftedness to the encounter, the result can be something intensely erotic for both partners.

Men, too, are more complex than we give them credit for. In my therapy work, I've heard from hundreds of men who have said they desire deep connection and badly want to be passionate lovers for their mates. But our culture denies boys and men so many years of touch and nurture by demanding that they suffocate their emotions; that they "man up" and toughen up, resisting any behavior that's thought to be even remotely feminine, such as love, nurture, self-expression, desire, intuition, wisdom, and touch. Consider that boys are typically removed from the laps of their caregivers at about age six, and the next time they're allowed to seek physical affection without stigma is when they're sexually active. No wonder men long for touch.

That's why it can be so freeing for a man to discover those qualities and skills in himself for the first time. My organization runs couples retreats, and men are often shocked at what a turn-on it can be for them to bring erotic, ecstatic pleasure to their wives—especially when their wives really let themselves show their own sexiness and creativity! It's popular to assume that men want sex and not relationships, and that women want relationships and not sex, but the reality is so much bigger, more complex, more fun than that: men and women each want both. They just have different ideas about what those things mean.

WHOSE PLEASURE?

Stacey's email suggested a sense of male entitlement in how she and Tyler had arranged their sex life. Clearly, there had been a dance going on—an unconscious, patriarchal understanding that Tyler was entitled to a certain kind of sex with a certain degree of frequency. I don't assume that he intended to act from a place of entitlement. But both Tyler and Stacey had marinated in a culture that led them to believe that Tyler was owed something. He was just doing what he thought guys do. He'd even done what the church had told him: he'd been a good boy—he'd waited until marriage to have intercourse; he'd subverted his bodily desires long enough and was now ready to enjoy this formerly forbidden experience.

Like so many women, Stacey had also received the message loud and clear, both from her upbringing in the church and from the culture, that sex was his to take, hers to give. It is a fundamentally patriarchal idea, similar to the notion that men cannot control their sexual desires and that women are responsible for men's physical advances. Women are to dress modestly; women are responsible for keeping themselves safe. It's no surprise that we're seeing the rise of the #MeToo movement, as women raise their voices against these messages and the ways such patriarchal assumptions have led to years of harassment, abuse, and assault against women.

The assumption that men are the recipients of sexual pleasure and women are the givers means that many men are never taught about things like sexual consent, how alcohol affects decision-making, or how power differentials work. Many women learn that their own pleasure and sexuality in the company of men is risky at best. And they learn that they don't have a say in what happens to their own bodies. The message that men can't control themselves and are entitled to sexual pleasure, regardless of their partner's desire, is real and insidious and dangerous to all involved.

In a marriage, these messages result in the relationship revolving around the man's emotions and reactivity, leaving no room for the woman to experience her own fulfillment in the exchange. Tyler and Stacey had gotten caught in a cycle that kept him in focus and her on the margins. It was a huge loss for each of them—a decade spent in a destructive dynamic, within nothing close to the egalitarian way of relating that could have meant a more enjoyable and varied erotic life for them both. It spelled the death of their marriage, just as it has for countless other couples.

The church has taught that sex is meant for marriage, which isn't problematic on its own. But it does imply that we are only properly sexual when we're partnered. In reality, we are sexual beings, partnered or not, and our sexuality grows with us throughout our lives. A healthy understanding of sexuality honors us, honors our partner (if there is one), and honors our values, all at once.

Whether or not you believe that sex is best practiced within marriage, it's important to understand that sexuality and desire are constant forces, and that we need to be intentional and caring in regard to our sexual selves. Knowing your sexual self—your desire and pleasure—is necessary for entering a sexual relationship as a full participant. Sexual expression between people who know themselves and are willing to communicate honestly—bringing their desires to one another—has the potential to constantly evolve and grow into something newer, fresher, freer. It requires maturity, sexual self-knowledge, and integrity. When those things are present throughout a relationship, the intimacy is qualitatively different.

Masters and Johnson, the legendary sexologists, once did a study of sexual behaviors among gay, lesbian, and heterosexual couples. They found that the couples who had the most varied sexual experiences—teasing, an expansive use of time, building of anticipation—were their gay and lesbian subjects. The straight couples reported fairly routine sex lives: no building of anticipation, no teasing, no fun. Just sex. End of story.[1]

Many of us sex therapists hear that exact story from our clients: One or both partners is bored to tears because the sexual relationship between them hasn't been tended. What they have instead is a systematic, predictable, and ultimately uninteresting sexual experience, and both partners are nearly asleep through it. When the culture and the church haven't provided tools or education for relational and sexual flourishing, each partner suffers from a failure of imagination. A couple yawning their way through boring sex can't even imagine questions like "What kind of touch does my body like?" or "Who determines what kind of sex the two of us have?" or "What's the next frontier for us in our exploration together?" Those are questions of creativity, playful experimentation, and enjoyment.

By the time she wrote me, Stacey was finally getting a chance to ask herself questions like those, and she was experiencing a great deal of freedom in the asking. How heartbreaking that no one bothered to teach her until she was in her thirties! Think of how different, how wonderful, her experience could have been if she had been guided to ask those questions during her growing-up years, through a developmentally appropriate sex-education program that included material on the "how" of relational intimacy. Think of how different Tyler's behavior could have been if he, too, had been given some basic grounding in how his wife's pleasure-systems worked, how the way she experienced sexual fulfillment was different from how he did. Think of the way their story could have gone if they'd known how much fun and intimacy they could have together.

The intimacy that a healthy sex life creates for a couple isn't just about sexual fulfillment, although that's a good goal. It's also about the benefits it holds for a relationship in general. I often ask my clients what they think the role of sexual intimacy is, outside of making babies. Why are we given sexual desire, anyway? They usually say something like "connection and pleasure," and almost nothing about specific positions or techniques. They usually say that the best sex happens when both partners have fun, feel close, and experience something that feels good, even if it's not the same each time, even if it's not intercourse. The emotional component of sex cannot be overstated.

Deeply attached relationships are complex, and the most complex dynamics take place only in our most attached relationships. Therefore, our greatest opportunities for emotional and erotic intelligence present themselves here in this place. I believe we're attracted to deeply attached relationships time and again, despite the challenges along the way, because at the heart of it, we're seeking to grow, to learn, to understand our own belovedness, and to understand the deep art of loving. These deeply attached relationships of partnership are also the places where we will struggle with our shame and reactivity. When we are known and loved as we truly are, we feel safe and secure in our relationships. When couples can remember they are both radically valuable and radically imperfect and come to each other—even in their hard times, in their fears, and mistakes—with the intent to connect and share pleasure, sexuality can be a healing balm.

REFRAMING SEXUALITY

I did some research into whether Judeo-Christian culture has ever been sex-positive. I knew that there had been a mind/body split that predated even Jesus' time, and even though Jesus himself was integrated, inclusive, and body-affirming in his ministry, the sexual ethic that evolved several centuries later was vastly more constrained. I wondered if there had ever been examples of body-affirmation in the church's heritage, and if so, how could we revive that heritage?

To my surprise, I found some amazing, body-celebrating threads woven through Hebrew scripture and Jewish mystical stories, revealing thousands of years of witness to a relentlessly loving God communicating a deep, even erotic love toward God's people. One discovery in particular convinced me that the Hebrew people had clearly understood how sexuality could flourish for both men and women.

I stumbled on a series of eight guidelines called the Vow of Onah, a wonderfully sex-positive series of affirmations based in Jewish law and tradition. The vow was taken by a Jewish man upon marriage and contained provisions like: "Sex should only be experienced in a time of joy. Sex for selfish personal satisfaction, without regard for the partner's pleasure, is wrong and evil." Another says, "Sex may never be used as a weapon against a partner, either by depriving sex or by compelling it." My favorite one says, "Sex is a woman's right, not a man's"—and that he is required to "learn her; to make sure that she experiences pleasure and joy each time they touch."[2]

What stuns me about that guideline isn't just that it runs counter to our Western, patriarchal way of thinking, but that it helps men and women in heterosexual relationships come to marriage with a mature understanding of sex and intimacy. When we raise men to be self-focused, it can take a man five decades before he begins to realize that the care and attention he gives his career works, too, in his relationships with his kids and partner. By midlife, men are often on their second families or in listless marriages, largely because they haven't been taught to prioritize sex and pleasure for their spouses earlier in life. Think of how many men might have been spared a lot of suffering at midlife if only they had known sooner!

The Vow of Onah carries benefits for women too. When we raise a woman to pay attention primarily to others, she'll often have to wait until she is in her fifties before she realizes that she matters, that she can say yes or no, that she is allowed to aknowledge her own needs and desires.

If we raise boys to pay attention to the important "others" in their lives as they are growing up, and raise girls to pay attention to how they themselves are treated and to recognize that they have a voice, it's vastly more likely that men and women will have more egalitarian and satisfying relationships by the time they reach their thirties. It can save them twenty years of waiting for the good stuff. The Vow of Onah may be hundreds of years old, but it's brilliant!

The Vow of Onah points to the idea that we never simply "have sex." We have to be ready for it in a way that is honest and true to ourselves. Stacey's email described the sense of expectation she felt from Tyler, and how it had become clear he expected her to prepare herself—trick herself—into being ready for sex and to act like it was what she wanted each time. What was missing was Tyler's awareness to say, "Honey, I see your reluctance. What's that about?"

Women tricking themselves into sexual engagement is nothing new, and I've even heard it advocated by well-meaning church leaders at retreats for Christian women. Part of the problem is that women in our culture have never been able to have sex in the way they want. Over the centuries, women have been so commodified, so oppressed, and so held back from access to real information about sexual health, that they have lost all sense that their pleasure or desires count. They've been bored and suffering, and they—we—have lost all vocabulary to own it and do anything about it. We've forgotten that we matter.

Research shows that when you ask women what makes them sexually satisfied, they typically say something like, "When my partner is satisfied and I'm not in pain." Notice that nothing in that account references a woman's own erotic pleasure. When desire comes from a sense of obligation, it's only natural that it will shrivel up and die over time. As soon as a sexual relationship turns into a transaction, desire disappears. Desire loves fun, connection, pleasure, authenticity, anticipation, and playfulness. It doesn't like to feel forced. It doesn't like predictability, unless it brings comfort.

Women in particular tend to want to be desired for who they are, not for what they can do for someone, and they can smell fakeness a mile away.

That doesn't mean, however, that desire doesn't like planning. Desire actually loves anticipation, which can involve many different kinds of setup in advance. The key is planning for fun—for what you desire, what you want. I advise couples to plan for sex like they plan a garden: taking time to "plant" what they enjoy tasting, smelling, touching. Couples need to nurture desire, water it, play in it, think creatively—and tend it like a bed of flowers.

And just as a garden thrives when we understand what each flower needs to grow and bloom, each partner needs to know their sexual self. That's key to offering ourselves to a partner. And listening—truly listening—to a partner's sexual self-knowing is the first step on the road to full, exotic, fulfilling sexual communication. It takes time to learn how to let desire flow through us and out of us toward our partners, and into us from the one who loves us. But that's what it takes to have connection and pleasure. That's the power and beauty of what sexuality in a marriage can be—something that thrills and fulfills both partners, allowing them to be the sexual beings that God created them to be. If we believe in marriage, if we hold to the idea that this is a sacred and holy union, the church would do well to provide parents, youth, and young adults with the tools to build a whole and healthy understanding of sexuality, and spare people the hardships that are so common in marriages today.

Now in her thirties and single, Stacey has been learning about the Hebrew erotic wisdom in her Christian heritage. She's been allowing herself the freedom to think differently about her body, to learn more about how it works and what it likes, to own her sexuality as part of who she is. "I love the idea that women were once understood to be where men would go to access the Divine," she wrote me recently. "My sexuality feels like that now. It feels like a blessed gift and a deep connection to the heart of a loving God. Never before have I had a place to say that aloud. I believe that God made me exactly the way I am—passionate, powerful, full of life, full of love." That's the gift of a sexually healthy relationship, a gift that both men and women deserve and need.

Dr. Tina Schermer Sellers is an educator, sex therapist, family therapist, speaker, author, consultant, and thought leader. She serves as an Associate Professor of Marriage & Family Therapy and Director of Medical Family Therapy at Seattle Pacific University. Dr. Sellers also founded the Northwest Institute on Intimacy, whose mission is to provide training in sex therapy and spiritual intimacy for psychotherapists and to provide a solid referral source to physicians, clergy, and community leaders.

ENDNOTES

1   Time Magazine, Monday, April 23, 1979. "Sexes. Masters and Johnson on Homosexuality. An exclusive preview of the famed sex researchers' newest study." http://content.time.com/time/magazine/article/0,9171,920282-2,00.html

2   It's almost impossible to cite a single source for this information. Like much of Jewish law, these ideas are a combination of written law, midrash, and interpretive works. I have done my best to distill these many voices into a concise explanation of this vow. For more information, please see any of the following:

    ↳   Moshe Idel, *Kabbalah and Eros* (New Haven: Yale University Press, 2005), 18, 147.

    ↳   Eduardo Pitchon, "Hasidic Attitudes Towards Sexuality," *Jewish Explorations of Sexuality*, ed. Jonathan Magonet (Providence: Berghahn, 1995), 205–212.

    ↳   Hannah Rockman, "Sexual Behaviour Among Ultra Orthodox Jews: A Review of Laws and Guidelines," in *Jewish Explorations of Sexuality*, ed. Jonathan Magonet (Providence: Berghahn, 1995), 191, 204.

    ↳   Tina Schermer-Sellers, *Sex, God, and the Conservative Church—Erasing Shame from Sexual Intimacy* (New York: Routlege Press, 2017), 73–78.

4

PINK CAPES AND ZIP-UP BOOTS

LANGUAGE, IDENTITY, AND THE POWER OF WORDS

BY ISAAC ARCHULETA

The summer before I entered kindergarten, I spent many hours with my favorite aunt, Sara. In addition to loving me wholeheartedly, my aunt had the most fabulous brown leather, zip-up boots. Wanting to imitate her spectacular style, I slipped on the wooden-heel-clanging, gold-zippered boots to prance up and down the driveway. Making a cape out of a pink blanket tied around my neck, I pretended to be the king of the empire. I felt empowered as the cape swayed in the wind. And those boots—they brought a sovereignty that my five-year-old body had never experienced. On that hot day in 1988, another part of my desire was born: a craving for agency.

But as my uncle and his exhaust-pumping Toyota turned up the drive, panic filled my body. Machismo was such a part of his Mexican heritage, and I was afraid I was going to be in trouble. Preparing for the backlash I would receive for wearing my aunt's boots and that pink blanket, I dashed for a secret corner in a faraway room. When my uncle saw me, he smirked. "Maricón," he spat. Certain the invective must have been slanderous, I later asked a neighbor what *maricón* meant. "Faggot," he told me.

A message about my desire had been communicated. As a little boy, I quickly learned that my expressions of gender were disgusting, worthy of a loved one's scorn. My innocent desire to be autonomous was tainted by the opinion of a man who was supposed to love me unconditionally. I had lost any trust in myself to be a good version of a boy. My desire for agency had transformed into self-doubt. The language used to characterize my behavior had, in fact, distorted the nature of my desire. My uncle had shamed my inherent desire for self-expression and healthy femininity, taking away something meant for beauty and intended to bring richness to the human experience.

Christianity has had a long-standing, ambivalent relationship with human desire. Ministers of many pulpits preach misleadingly about desire, as though it is the bedrock of sin. Many people walk out of churches armed to defend their righteousness against the cravings of their own hearts. The confusing part is that love, sexuality, and authenticity are all characteristics of God's intentional design for human beings. Many theologians would claim that we were made to be reciprocating beings, living in relationship with others.[1] To be relational necessitates love—one of the prominent desires of the heart. Jesus himself said that to love is the primary commandment (Matthew 22:36-40). Why then do the Christian language and the Christian cultural ethos shape not only a negative view of our desires, but also the manner in which we subconsciously withhold them?

One of the very first mentions of desire in the biblical text occurs while Eve is being punished for indulging in the enticing, yet sinful, fruit (Genesis 3:16). We read that as a result, her desires will be for her husband and he will rule over her—her role will be one of constant subservience. In this case, desire seems to be a pawn used against Eve, a tormentor reeling from within her very own body. But from Genesis we travel through only a few centuries of historical texts to find a book of poems in which we read the wonderful language of a creative and emotionally astute psalmist. Our desires are from God, the psalmist tells us (Psalm 37:4). The Old Testament, it seems, leaves us with a rather dualistic and complex view of human desire.

The popular New Testament renegade, the apostle Paul, adds some rather dramatic contributions to the discourse on human desire. Galatians 5:17 gives us the quintessential rhetoric Paul used to divide our human desires into two halves. It reads, "For what the flesh desires is opposed to the Spirit, and what the Spirit desires is opposed to the flesh; for these are opposed to each other, to prevent you from doing what you want." Pitting the human body against its behavior, Paul uses very direct language elsewhere, too, to define the differences between the flesh and the Spirit (Romans 8:5; Galatians 5:16; Galatians 5:24; Ephesians 2:3, 4:22; Colossians 3:5). Like a good author paying attention to his audiences, Paul uses a variety of terms throughout his epistles to create a major distinction between humanity's fallibility and the cleansing mechanisms of righteousness. It's easy to extrapolate from Paul's ancient letters that righteousness requires the denial of fleshly desires. But all of our desires are God-given, are they not?

What do we make of Psalm 37:4, where we read, "Take delight in the LORD, and he will give you the desires of your heart"? I used to think God was much like Santa Claus. After pining for a best friend, I hoped God would deliver him like a present under the tree on Christmas morning. Now, however, I see that God gives us the yearnings—such as for belonging, connectedness, and camaraderie—that underscore the hope for that best friend.

Tucked into the language of the Bible are indications both that our desires are our own enemy (Romans 6:12) and that they come directly from God (Psalm 37:4). Although I wish there were a simple resolution to this duality, I'm afraid the message we find in Scripture depicts human reality rather well. The complexity of our human desire originates, I suggest, from shame's ability to wrap itself around our desires. Shame is the true culprit, not our desire.

LANGUAGE CONSUMPTION

Sadly, the messages of shame are passed down from parent to child, from minister to congregant, from society to community member. Language is the conveyor belt sending shame's messages straight to the core of our identities. Whether through the biblical discourse or the socializing language of a loving parent, shame weaves its way into the fabric of our desire, ultimately creating a blanket that covers our authentic selves.

Even with the purest intentions, many parents use language to mold their children's desires into socially acceptable behaviors. A parent wanting a "tough" son may tell him that men don't cry and to not act "like a girl." After hearing words like *sissy* and *mama's boy*, a young boy starts to characterize his innate proclivities for emotional sensitivity and nurture as weak or inappropriate. After abandoning anything that categorizes his emotional expressions as lady-like or feminine, he seeks refuge in a world of emotional isolation that feels like toughness. Women and femininity, for this developing young man, become subservient to his maleness. He will learn to interpret his own femininity—and "female" emotional responses—not as beautiful, but as less-than. As he internalizes these messages about the value of feminine qualities, he propagates the pollination of psychological patriarchy in his heart and his behavior. He is now a host that plays along by degrading sentimentality, femaleness, and femininity.

It doesn't stop there. Many mothers burned by men will train their daughters to be emotional islands, creating an anti-dependent daughter. Although I completely agree that women do not *need* men, many of these daughters feel like they betray themselves and their mothers when they fall in love with a man. These daughters have lost the sense of beauty about falling in love and may feel they are betraying themselves by wanting healthy interdependence. Instead of learning how to express their needs and wants in healthy ways *inside* the context of relationships, they have been conditioned to abandon their own needs and wants, their own cravings for connectedness. They, too, see toughness and emotional numbness as preferable to softness and emotional vulnerability. Again, we see the dissemination of psychological patriarchy. The degree to which many of us subconsciously participate in the derogation of women and femininity—and empower maleness and masculinity—is both astounding and deeply disturbing.

Language shapes how we carry our own desires. The language we consume, specifically from those we trust or those to whom we wish to belong, helps determine whether we suppress, deny, acknowledge, or even celebrate our emotional desires. Little do we know that the language we use and consume has the power not only to classify our emotional cravings and add shame to our own sense of self, but also to distort our relational roles.

THE EGO SPLIT

The shame that is nurtured by experiences like the one I had as a young child in my cape and boots creates what psychotherapists call the ego split. The ego split develops over time as various emotional cravings (such as the craving for agency) are boxed up and labeled dirty. Although my example may be more dramatic than most, ego splitting occurs in our daily lives even when we're not aware of it. For example, when a hungry child pleads for a snack and an angry caretaker barks with frustration, the child subtly internalizes the belief that her needs are an annoyance, especially if the parent's angry response is the norm. Likewise, if a transgender teen hears undeniable transphobic theological messages, the cravings of authenticity and the desire to express their identity will be an experience of shame—one that settles deeply in a transgender teen's psyche. Rather than learning how to assert their voice and self-advocate in a healthy manner, the adolescent's involuntary yearning for authentic gender expression feels like it's inherently in opposition to God. It's only a matter of time before a child with an ego split in the area of gender identity believes that they are inherently flawed.

Ego splitting segregates our desires into two categories: clean and dirty. And much of this categorization is shaped by the words we use to talk about them. As loved ones and friends watch us express our genuine personalities, they have the option to give us positive or negative feedback. Sometimes feedback is a verbal reaction of praise or condemnation, but it can also appear in the form of a smile or a disapproving look. Of course, ego splitting is a very subtle and subconscious process. Eventually, any child will take the inconspicuous socialization provided by their parents and loved ones as a sign to mold their desires into what they believe to be an acceptable moral framework.

For instance, taking the harmful claims of purity culture, a young adult might feel that any desire for sexual activity before marriage offends God. They might, therefore, create a shame-based sexual ethic that has more to do with self-repression and self-hatred than with Christian morality. In other words, ego splitting allows shame to feel like morality. For instance, if I believe my desire for sexual activity before marriage is proof of a God-opposing desire in my body, I'll feel empowered—even righteous—when I successfully suppress the craving. We think that the angel whispering in our ear has won the battle. But in fact, the wiles of evil have tricked us from the inside out.

This is where shame is in cahoots with our self-righteousness. Shame distorts our normal emotional desires and asks us to celebrate overcoming what others have labeled dirty. But so-called dirty desires eventually bubble up to the surface, creating a compulsive reaction—the kinds of behavior that can only be executed in the private, shameful corners of our lives. Thus, we soothe ourselves with the very thing that shames us. This is to say that when we have a bad relationship with our desire, we also have a bad relationship with our behavior.

At the same time, the desires that have been deemed "clean" are paraded around. We come to believe that socially approved or "righteous" desires are the pillars of godly living. We use our clean desires to motivate behaviors that become the spackling for one spectacular façade. Many authors, like David Benner and Father Richard Rohr,[2] call this façade the false self. Essentially, we have learned what earns praise. Subconsciously we will pull the clean desires into the foreground of our public lives as a means of manufacturing relational, spiritual, and social capital. They allow us to fabricate acceptance. We leave the dirty desires tucked behind the backdrop of our lives, leaving us feeling ashamed that they exist in us at all.

SHAME'S DISTORTIONS

The original definition of *sin* comes from the Hebrew word *hamartia*, meaning "to miss the mark."[3] I find this peculiar and ironic, particularly when we're talking about desire. For example, we see many instances where Paul makes a big deal out of human behavior. Using language to characterize human desires as either clean or dirty, Paul seems to land at either admonishing or praising physical behaviors (Ephesians 4:22; Romans 12:1). We conflate his use of *hamartia* with behavior, thinking that to sin is to miss the behavioral benchmark of righteousness.

Using decisive language, Paul completes one of the most widespread theologies of ego splitting. Juxtaposing the mindset of fear with the mindset of the Spirit (Romans 8:15-16 and setting the flesh in opposition to the Spirit (Galatians 5:17), Paul seems to require ego splitting. But what if we have misunderstood and erroneously exegeted Paul's words in a way that leaves us emotionally starving in our everyday lives?

As a young seminarian I fell in love with the sentiments of Philippians 1:20. It reads, "It is my eager expectation and hope that I will not be put to shame in any way, but that by my speaking with all boldness, Christ will be exalted now as always in my body, whether by life or by death." I applied the words Paul wrote to my daily life. I hoped they would help me fight the same-sex attractions that burgeoned throughout my body. Suffering from a massive ego split, I learned that my desires to belong and to feel affection were clean when applied to woman and family, but dirty when oriented toward men to whom I was attracted.

I thought that God could only be exalted in my body if I denied the flesh and showed disdain for any desires that were of the body. The belief that my same-sex desires were dirty meant I couldn't trust the involuntary desire that comprised my sexual orientation. Finding "sufficient courage" to denounce my desires and let God be exalted in my body meant that I had to hate the desire for male-to-male affection and belonging. I vowed that "by life or by death," I would not take part in any behavior that left me shamed before God.

I was determined to please God even if it meant hating myself. I believed it wasn't enough to avoid the behaviors; it was my self-denial and self-hatred that would inspire God's forgiveness. Creating one spectacular show of shame for God would surely win me favor and reinforce my value, or so I thought. I had created an illusion of earning value by performing for God.

THE ILLUSION OF CONTROL

One Christmas I was sitting in a busy food court watching all the shoppers dash for their last-minute gifts. A mother and her four-year-old daughter settled at a small table, and the mother handed the young girl a bottle of orange juice. As the child twisted the bottle open, the mother instructed her daughter to avoid spilling the juice. Needless to say, within seconds there was orange juice pouring from the bottle and dripping to the ground. In an angry and embarrassed tone, the mother reprimanded the little girl, "I told you not to spill your orange juice!"

Immediately, the girl's face reddened and she shrank in her chair. Here's what was going on: the mother promoted the illusion that her daughter's childish behavior was maddening, rather than acknowledging the restrictions of a four-year-old's capabilities. In other words, the mother shamed her daughter for being a child with still-developing coordination and motor skills. The mother's body language, angry tone, and verbal reprimand communicated to the daughter that it was her behavior that made her mother so mad. The little girl experienced a striking *whoosh* of the illusion of control.

The illusion of control is a phenomenon I have come to notice in our everyday lives, as well as in the ways we approach God. The illusion lives in our assumption that we can control another's emotional disposition. I mention it here because the illusion of control is disseminated by the language we use. When this pattern persists, children inevitably begin to believe that they are valueless, precisely because their innocent behaviors and benign mistakes cause others to be disappointed. Eventually, the shaming belief will stand as an identity: "I am something disappointing."

The devastating effects of the combination of the ego split and the illusion of control leave children believing they have to earn value by performing for others, that they need to sublimate themselves to ensure that others are pleased with them. When we perpetuate the illusion that children are in control of our happiness, approval, or mood, we give them the impression that their authenticity is unwelcomed at best, and offensive at worst. Because language has taught them that 1) their desires can be dirty, and 2) they are in control of another's fickle emotional dispositions, they live trapped in the role of performer, hiding whole parts of themselves in an effort to become safe and valuable. Eventually the child leaves authenticity behind and assumes the role of a lifelong performer, perpetually hunting for the behaviors that lead to acceptance and avoiding those that lead to rejection.

The apostle Paul gave us some incredible language that we have used to initiate the illusion of control. It is easy to access sermons that preach how our behavior *makes* God angry. We speak of ourselves as a spotted bride scouring for ways to make ourselves clean. With language such as "lukewarm" (Revelation 3:16) and "backslider," we have acquiesced to the idea that the illusion of control is in fact reality. We assume, that by means of our own behavior, we—not God—control God's fluctuating appraisals of our personhood. The illusion of control strips God of any autonomy and all sovereignty. In this light, we feel incredibly comfortable having performed well for God, leaving God with no other option but to give us a standing ovation. The genuine desires that fuel authenticity are completely lost, but we feel at home in our costumes.

All of this brings us back to language. The words we wield are our best weapon in destroying another person's identity. Language can be a devastating tool, like a craftsman's blade that shaves layers upon layers from the tree's form.

Take, for example, the parents of a trans teen who is just coming out. Although many parents in this situation are stricken with grief and fear, their unrelenting or forgetful use of given pronouns (*he* and *him* or *she* and *her*) or deadnaming (using the child's given name, rather than their newly chosen one) can be devastating for their teen. After years of stabilizing the illusion of control by performing as the cisgender child, the coming-out process—and the parents' denial of it—will feel like a massive ego split, leaving the child feeling utterly invisible, but also drenched in failure. They have failed at maintaining the performance of being cis, thereby failing at keeping their transphobic parents happy.

STRIPPED FROM THE IMAGO DEI

There's a wonderful book called *Simply Bonaventure* that brings life to the profound thoughts of a thirteenth-century Franciscan monk. It includes a discussion on language that's helpful in this conversation, particularly his ideas on "Word."[4] Bonaventure claimed that the best name for Christ was "Word." Before Jesus walked among us, he was part of God's consciousness, an all-details-included *Word* (John 1:1). Rather than trying to deduce information about the Christ, Bonaventure claimed, we should meditate on the "Word" that originated in the consciousness of God for the most precise understanding of who Jesus was and is.

Making a connection between Bonaventure's "Word" and Genesis 1:26-27, where God makes humankind in the image of God, it's clear that we all bear the image and likeness of God. We were and still are that eternal "Word" in the consciousness of God. Theologians use the term *imago Dei* to describe this understanding of humanity—we are literally the image of God. But with the ego splitting and the illusion of control that shape us—not to mention the ways in which our language contributes to the ego splitting and illusion of control in the people we love—the imago Dei becomes distorted over time.

Language has the power not only to recategorize our emotional cravings, but to rob us of knowing our inherent value, our original design. This is a massive identity distortion in which we lose the opportunity to know who we were created to be, the original Word, the bearers of God's image.

REPAIRING THE LANGUAGE

What would it have been like for me to know that original Word, that all-encompassing, Isaac Archuleta–forming imago Dei? What would it be like for you? Knowing the divine essence of our identities before they became flesh and blood would be remarkable. I venture to say that we have strayed far from God's original intentions. The language we use and its subconscious effects leave us mimicking our authentic selves rather than beholding them.

I want to circle back around to Philippians 1:20 for a minute. Remember how I used to read that verse? It was full of the illusion of control, the thinking that I could in some way control God's love for me by how effectively I denied myself. If I was courageous enough to deny the "desires of the flesh" (1 Peter 2:11), I would be shameless, leaving room for God to be exalted in my body. But I read it wrong. If we strip away the ego split and the illusion of control, Philippians becomes an entirely new passage.

What if the courage Paul spoke of was not about having the willpower to avoid ourselves but the courage to be ourselves? In fact, I believe that Paul was referring to a courage that could and should overcome the ego split and deconstruct the illusion of control. I now read Philippians 1:20 as an affirmation that I am God's created child and that there is only one expectation of me: to be authentic. Reclaiming my God-created authenticity deconstructs the pillars that bolster the ego split and frees me to be the living expression of God's emotional desire, rather than believing I control it. Let me give you my updated version of Philippians 1:20: "I eagerly expect and hope that I will in no way fall victim to the ego split and the illusion of control, but will have sufficient courage to be authentic, so that now as always Christ's original Word for who I am will be exalted in my body, whether by life or by death." Undoing the power of shame allows us to rewrite our stories. Now, that is a bombastic way of using language!

Of course, if we plan to be agents of the gospel, we have to be aware of our use of language. To raise healthy, well-adjusted adults who live stabilized in their identity as the imago Dei, we must be prepared to preserve their identities, which in many ways means we must protect them from our own ego-splitting immaturity and shame.

I am convinced that to hit the mark (to be without sin) means that we have integrated the desires called dirty into the clean pile, not because we don't care about our behaviors, but because we have seen their innocence once again. We have to have courage to reclaim those parts of ourselves that were once wrapped in shame, allowing them to return to their God-given state of goodness. To have a healthy relationship with desire means that we will have a healthy relationship with behavior.

There is no doubt in my mind that beneath all behaviors, those considered moral and those considered immoral, are all underscored by an innocent emotional craving. The language, however, that wraps shame around our desires distorts the ways in which we satisfy each particular craving. In this light, having sufficient courage means asserting that we are not dirty, that we are in fact a spotless bride, not because we have performed a spectacular show for God, but because our very design as the imago Dei is spotless.

Isaac Archuleta is the Executive Director of Spiritual and Relational Formation for Q Christian Fellowship. Isaac has spent time as a seminary professor and now owns a counseling practice devoted to the LGBTQIA community and their religious families, specifically to help those navigating the road he's journeyed. Isaac has a Master of Arts in Clinical Mental Health Counseling. He is invited to speak at conferences, churches, and forums across the nation, contributes to The Huffington Post, and hosts weekend seminars for couples, individuals, and religious parents of children in the LGBTQIA community. Isaac's pronouns are he/him/his.

ENDNOTES

1   Jack O. Balswick, Pamela Ebstyne King, and Kevin S. Reimer, *The Reciprocating Self: Human Development in Theological Perspective* (Downers Grove, Ill: InterVarsity Press, 2005).

2   See Benner's *The Gift of Being Yourself: The Sacred Call to Self-Discovery* (Downers Grove, IL: IVP, 2015) and Rohr's *Falling Upward: A Spirituality for the Two Halves of Life* (San Francisco: Jossey-Bass, 2011).

3   James Henry Thayer. *A Greek-English Lexicon of the New Testament: Being Grimm's Wilke's Clavis Novi Testamenti* (New York: American Book Co., 1889).

4   Ilia Delio, *Simply Bonaventure: An Introduction to His Life, Thought, and Writings*, 2nd ed., (Hyde Park, NY: New City Press, 2013).

5

WHAT DOES IT MEAN TO BE TRANSGENDER?

MOVING BEYOND BATHROOM BILLS AND INTO THE LIVES OF REAL PEOPLE

BY REV. DR. PAULA STONE WILLIAMS

A note from the author: *I have written and spoken extensively about my life as a transgender woman. Here, I offer some reflections from my story as a framework for the scientific information that can help those who are new to this conversation get a better understanding of what it means—and does not mean—to be a transgender person.*

I was an inquisitive four-year-old living in Huntington, West Virginia, the child of a fundamentalist pastor, when I first knew I was transgender. At the time, I had no name for it. Like a character in Ursula K. LeGuin's novel, The Left Hand of Darkness, *I thought I could change from one gender to another. I was confident I would be able to begin kindergarten as the female I knew myself to be. But alas, changing genders was not as easy as I imagined, and I started school as a boy. I was not happy.*

While the word *transgender* might be a fairly recent addition to our cultural conversations, the existence of transgender people is not new at all. We have been around since the beginning of recorded history, but there has never been a time in which the transgender community has been as visible as we are today. As transgender people gain more visibility in the media, in politics, and in our local communities, it is important for people to have a clear understanding of what it means to be transgender. Let's start with some general terminology.

In the English lexicon, the term *transgender* has replaced the more archaic "transvestite" and "transsexual." A transvestite is a person who dresses in the clothing of the opposite sex, but wants to remain in the gender of his or her birth. A transsexual is someone whose gendered body is not in agreement with their expressed gender. Both are now identified in the *Diagnostic and Statistical Manual of Mental Disorders, Fifth Edition* (DSM-5) as having *gender dysphoria*. According to the DSM-5, "Individuals with gender dysphoria have a marked incongruence between the gender they have been assigned (usually at birth, referred to as *natal gender*) and their experienced/ expressed gender."[1]

When we're born, our gender is assigned based on the appearance of external genitalia. A *cisgender* individual is someone who remains comfortable in the gender identified at birth. The vast majority of people are cisgender. A *transgender* person is someone who identifies with the gender other than the one on their birth certificate. As the person's identity emerged, they began to identify with a different gender. So a transgender woman is someone who was identified as male at birth, but now identifies as female. A transgender man is a person who was identified as female at birth, but now identifies as male.

Drag queens are not transgender. They are men who enjoy dressing as females in public for fun and spectacle. Cross-dressers are men who enjoy wearing women's clothing for personal or sexual pleasure. Neither cross-dressers nor drag queens have a desire to live full time as members of the opposite sex. Their interest is confined to an occasional expression of femininity.[2]

There are also people who are *intersex*, having biological markers of both the male and female genders. According to the Intersex Society of North America, the most common intersex conditions are Congenital Adrenal Hyperplasia, Androgen Insensitivity Syndrome, Testosterone Biosynthetic Defects, and Klinefelter Syndrome.

Clearly, there's a lot of ground to cover as it relates to gender and biology, sex and identity, but I'm going to limit our discussion to issues related to gender dysphoria.

TRANSGENDER IDENTITY: A PRIMER

Gender dysphoria is a relatively rare condition, affecting 0.58 percent of the population.[3] Despite a number of ongoing studies, there is still no clear cause of gender dysphoria, but we do know what *doesn't* cause a person to be transgender: There are no post-birth reasons a person is transgender, no parenting decisions, no circumstantial events. Treating a small boy as though he is a girl or vice versa does not cause a child to be transgender.

There are some indications that the condition is genetic. A 2013 study looked at forty-three sets of twins in which at least one twin had already been identified as transgender. Among fraternal twins, there were no cases in which the sibling was also transgender. However, among the identical twins, 20 percent had a twin who was also transgender.[4] Though the study is small, it is one indication of a possible prenatal or genetic cause of gender dysphoria.

A person's gender is determined at the time of conception, when a sperm contributes either an X or a Y chromosome to the X chromosome of an egg. For most of the first trimester of pregnancy, internal structures of an XX (biological female) or XY (biological male) fetus are identical. At the end of the first trimester, an XY fetus receives an androgen wash that causes the fetus to develop the reproductive organs of a male. It's not until the beginning of the third trimester, however, that the brain develops connections to the body that has been created. One hypothesis is that in transgender people, there is some kind of developmental interruption in the second trimester that causes the brain to make an incomplete connection to the body that has been created.

Interestingly, gender dysphoria is not the only condition that results from an unusual brain-body connection. There is a rare condition known as *apotemnophilia* in which the brain does not make a connection to a limb of the body. The limb is perceived to be a foreign object. If you or I were to lose a limb, we would have a phantom limb: our brain would still be wired to believe a limb was in place, and we would sometimes experience sensations as if it were there. But if a person with apotemnophilia loses a limb, his or her brain will experience relief, since the brain never made a connection to the limb in the first place.[5] Some suggest a similar condition might lie behind gender dysphoria.

Another potential cause of gender dysphoria is medications taken by mothers during pregnancy. Mothers who took DES, a drug given between the 1930s and the 1970s to stop miscarriages, gave birth to sons who were far more likely to be transgender than the population at large. That is one possible reason there are almost twice as many natal males (65 percent) who are transgender, as natal females (35 percent).[6]

In 2018, I consulted with the NPR show *Radiolab* for their "Gonads" series on sexual development. As the series unfolded, it was fascinating to see the clear science of how we become gendered beings, as well as the definable interruptions in the process that result in people who are intersex. The science on why we are transgender, however, is not nearly as clear.

Having no firm scientific understanding of why we are transgender is a source of frustration to many transgender people. Better understanding of causation would provide some level of personal comfort as we navigate the difficult waters of gender dysphoria. Better understanding of the causes of gender dysphoria would also help friends and family adjust to the news that a loved one is transgender.

People often equate gender identity with sexual identity. They are, in fact, two separate subjects. Put simply, your gender identity is who you want to go to bed *as*, and your sexual identity is whom you want to go to bed *with*. People often assume transgender women are attracted to males and transgender men are attracted to females. The reality is far more complex.

About 60 percent of transgender females are attracted to females, while 40 percent are attracted to males or identify as bisexual.[7] One should never make an assumption that just because someone is a transgender woman, she will be attracted to people of one gender or another. Fewer studies have been completed on the sexual identities of transgender men. We do know, however, that the majority of transgender men are attracted to females. Asking a transgender person about their sexual identity is not appropriate. Most of us prefer our sexual lives to remain private, and transgender individuals are no exception.

Some people identify as gender non-binary, or genderqueer, meaning they don't identify with either the male or female gender. Sixty-one percent of those who identify this way are between the ages of eighteen and twenty-four.[8] We obviously don't know if these individuals will continue to identify as non-binary as they grow older. We also don't know if these age-related statistics are an indicator of an increase in the number of non-binary adults, or if they will eventually choose to identify as male or female.

We are a binary society, and presenting as non-binary is particularly difficult when it comes to language. Many non-binary people prefer the pronouns "ze" and "zer" instead of "he" and "her," or "they" as a singular pronoun.[9] The use of appropriate pronouns is an important signifier for transgender and non-binary people who, like everyone else, want to be seen and named for who they are, not for who others might think they are. Using pronouns and other gender language carefully and well is one of the many ways people of faith can show care and support for transgender and genderqueer people.

STRESS AND SAFETY

While I knew I was transgender from early childhood, I never breathed a word to anyone. I grew up in the church and I knew better than to tell anyone about my true self. There was rarely a day I did not pray that I would wake up the next morning as a girl, but I had no one with whom I could speak about my frustration with the body I inhabited. I didn't hate being a boy. I just knew I wasn't one. I was as comfortable with boys as I was with girls, and exhibited no outward appearance of someone dealing with gender dysphoria. But deep inside, I knew I was a female.

During elementary school, I experienced few disruptions because of my gender dysphoria. But when puberty arrived I became deeply troubled. I hated the changes taking place in my body and desperately wanted to experience the changes taking place in the bodies of my female friends. I knew I was attracted to girls, but I also wanted to be the girls to whom I was attracted. That was a problem.[10]

By my high school years I had made some level of peace with my struggle and became convinced marriage would change my circumstances. When it didn't, I knew it was time to begin therapy.

Over the next several decades I worked hard to maintain my equilibrium and manage my gender dysphoria. I did not want my family to suffer. There came a point, however, when I realized that if I didn't transition, I might not survive. I told my children, and their painful journey began.

Within a week of coming out as transgender, I was totally unemployed. I had been with one Christian ministry for thirty-five years and had served as CEO for more than twenty years, leading the ministry through a period of unprecedented growth. I never had a bad review, but was fired within seven days. In twenty-one states you cannot be fired for being transgender, but in all fifty you can be fired if you are transgender and work for a religious corporation.

Because of my evangelical work environment, I knew thousands of people. In the five years after I came out, I heard supportive words from fewer than sixty of my former coworkers, and was visited by fewer than twenty. Only seven saw me more than once. I was fortunate that almost all of my non-evangelical friends remained by my side. Those friendships were crucial to my well-being through the first difficult years.

Thus began a period of incredible difficulty for my entire family. Our lives would never be the same.

The psychological stress of being transgender is tremendous. Forty percent of transgender people attempt suicide at some point in their lives, a rate seven times higher than with any other DSM diagnosis.[11] The reasons for serious suicidal ideation are clear. The 2015 US Transgender Study surveyed 27,715 transgender individuals and identified three major causes of suicidal ideation among the transgender population:

1. It is common for a transgender person to be rejected by family and friends. Many lose their entire support network when they come out, experiencing loneliness and isolation at a time when they are incredibly vulnerable. Humans are social creatures, and without a community, it's difficult to keep one's equilibrium, especially in a time of change and stress. More than half (54 percent) of transgender people have unsupportive families.

2. There are significant safety issues for transgender people. Forty-seven percent of transgender people have been sexually assaulted. Twenty-nine percent live in poverty, and only 16 percent own a home. While 40 percent have actually attempted suicide, 82 percent have seriously considered it. 24 percent have been physically abused by a partner.

   Transgender individuals who still carry visual or auditory clues of their previous gender report higher levels of rejection, harassment, violence, and physical and sexual abuse than those who "pass" in their new gender—those who are able to travel in public without being seen as transgender report no more social difficulties than the population at large.

The risks are highest for transgender women. Most people don't realize transgender men are, in fact, transgender. The effects of testosterone on a female body are more substantive than the effects of estrogen and anti-androgens on a male body. As a result, transgender men have fewer problems with overt prejudicial behavior than do transgender women. This is one reason transgender women are willing to go to great lengths to gain a more feminine appearance via facial feminization surgery, a tracheal shave, breast augmentation, electrolysis, and other procedures.

3. One of the greatest causes of suicidal ideation is the internalization of transphobia. When a person is under a constant barrage of attacks because of their basic identity, they suffer great psychological distress. This is a problem for transgender people who are out, but also for those who are not out, since they hear the unfiltered prejudicial comments of others.

   Transphobia is common among members of ethnic and religious groups that are less supportive of transgender people. Transgender individuals within those groups face a greater risk of suicidal ideation, particularly if they are adolescents. The evangelical Christian response to gender dysphoria is significantly more negative than the response of the population at large. Conservative faith communities are rarely supportive of transgender members. While 62 percent of transgender people identify themselves as religious or spiritual, 35 percent have left their religious communities because of the transphobia they encountered there.[12]

IN SEARCH OF SUPPORT

I was in college before I found anyone with whom I could speak about my deep desire to live as a female—it was a college professor who proved to be the thoughtful and accepting presence I needed. Because I lived in a religious world in which psychotherapy was viewed as unacceptable, it was another twelve years before I began therapy. For the next couple of decades I worked with a wonderful therapist who helped me navigate the shoals of my family of origin, my own family, my sexuality, and my gender identity.

While everything else got better and I felt confidently differentiated from my family and the expectations of those relationships, my gender dysphoria continued to get worse. I began taking estrogen and anti-androgens. I was hoping a low dose of hormonal treatment might be enough to help me make it through my life as a male.

Three months after beginning hormones, I returned to my prescribing physician. She said, "Oh my, your body is responding to this stuff like you're thirteen. You can stay on a low dose, but even at that level your body is going to begin exhibiting physical signs that will make your current life difficult to maintain." My own body was telling me I needed to transition.

After I came out, I lost almost all of my evangelical friends, and none of my non-evangelical friends. Unfortunately, the majority of those non-evangelical friends lived on the other side of the country. Cathy, my former wife, was my greatest source of comfort. But she was also going through her own pain, and I needed close friends in whom I could confide. While there were a number of wonderful friends during those trying years, there were none more important than my two co-pastors at Left Hand Church in Longmont, Colorado: Jen and Aaron. My close friends Christy and David were also always available during those times of great joy and deep sorrow.

Good friends and allies often mean the difference between life and death for a transgender person. Without those deep and abiding friendships, I do not know what I would have done.

Imagine waking up tomorrow morning and finding that while you slept, your body had changed genders. Most people would be extremely distressed. We are gendered beings in a gendered society. To be thrust into a new body, a new social reality, and a new cultural experience would be profoundly disturbing. The fact that none of it would be congruent with your self-understanding would be unbearable. That is the experience of a transgender person every single morning, as he or she begins another day in a body that feels foreign.

Supportive friends and family are crucial to keeping transgender people alive. A transgender person who has a positive coming-out experience has a far greater chance of thriving than do those who are greeted with rejection. They know there is at least one person in whom they can confide who will be sympathetic to their journey. A person coming to grips with his or her gender dysphoria also benefits from professional help, beginning with a therapist who is knowledgeable about gender dysphoria and sympathetic to those who identify as transgender. My experience is that therapists with an evangelical Christian background are less likely to provide helpful therapy to transgender clients. Some even focus on reparative therapy, utilizing modalities that have been used, without positive effect, on gay and lesbian clients. Fortunately, those therapies are now banned in an increasing number of states. To find a qualified therapist, I highly recommend looking for someone who is a member of WPATH (World Professional Association of Transgender Health) or in agreement with the principles of WPATH.

I believe it's in the best interest of a transgender person to seek professional counseling before doing any kind of medical intervention such as hormone therapy. It is absolutely essential if the transgender individual is a child or adolescent. Some providers within the medical community do not follow the guidelines of WPATH. They don't believe that working with a professional counselor should be a necessary qualifying experience for those seeking hormone therapy. Instead, they operate via informed consent, the process by which a patient is informed of the outcomes that can be expected with medical intervention, but without the requirement that the patient receive a defined period of psychological care before hormones are prescribed. I do not believe informed consent is an adequate replacement for therapy with a licensed mental health practitioner.

For some people with gender dysphoria, professional counseling might be the only care necessary. With the help of supportive friends and family and an excellent therapist, they are able to remain in the gender of their birth. Some people will be able to remain in their birth gender for a long time without unbearable distress. Some might be able to live their whole lives that way. If a person is able to remain within gender of their birth and still thrive, that's an option worth pursuing—transitioning has a massive impact on everyone within the social circle of a transgender person, which is part of why therapy is so important. The fact remains, however, that many who experience gender dysphoria will eventually decide that transitioning is their only viable option for a meaningful life.

TRANSFORMATION

Many transgender individuals feel the need to transition for their own psychological, spiritual, and physical health. This is when medical intervention becomes necessary. The first step is to consult with an endocrinologist or other physician who specializes in the treatment of transgender individuals. If the physician operates according to the standards of WPATH, they will require a letter from a licensed therapist certifying that the patient has been in therapy for a minimum of one year.

Hormone therapy is the most common medical intervention. Natal males are prescribed anti-androgens that stop the production of testosterone. Conjointly they receive estradiol that begins to make their bodies appear more feminine. Muscle mass decreases. Fat migrates from the waist to the hips, thighs, buttocks, and upper arms. Body hair transforms from a male pattern to the fine vellus hair common to females. Breast tissue begins to develop—the younger the client, the greater the impact of hormonal treatment on breast development. Skin becomes softer and the metabolism slows. All of the changes that are likely to occur will happen within four to five years of a person taking anti-androgens and estrogen. For many transgender people, no further treatment is desired.

For those who want to transition further, there are surgical options that can dramatically alter a transgender woman's physical appearance. Often, the first procedure is facial feminization surgery, in which facial features are made to more closely resemble a female face. This surgery can include a reduction of the forehead skeletal structure, reshaping of the chin, rhinoplasty, shortening the distance between the upper lip and the nose, and other feminizing procedures. At the same time as facial feminization is completed, most patients will also have a tracheal shave, in which the "Adam's apple" is shaved down to no longer protrude from the neck. The transgender treatment that takes the longest to complete is electrolysis. Facial hair does not change with hormonal treatment. Therefore a transgender woman will undergo up to a decade of laser therapy and/or electrolysis to rid her body of facial hair.

The reason transgender women frequently seek facial feminization surgery before any other is because the human brain takes its strongest cue about the gender from looking at faces. If a face appears decidedly male, we conclude the person is a male. If a face appears decidedly female, we conclude the person is a female. But if the face is seen as neutral, the human brain will usually see that face as male. Whether that's cultural conditioning or hardwiring is hard to say, but it is an unfortunate reality for transgender women to deal with. Changing one's facial structure is a big step in the transition from male to female.

Many transgender women who choose to surgically transition will have breast augmentation. A male rib cage is significantly larger than a female rib cage. Even though hormones may create breast tissue roughly the same size as that of natal females, the larger rib cage causes the breasts to appear smaller on a transgender woman. Breast augmentation makes the breasts more in proportion to the upper torso.

There are no medical procedures that raise the pitch of a transgender woman's voice. She must train her voice to use a higher pitch and find resonance in her head, not her chest. It's an ongoing process yielding varied results. Some transgender women sound like cisgender women, while others are never able to sound like anything but an adult male.

The most complex surgical procedure undergone by some transgender women is the removal of the testes and the utilization of the skin of the penis to create a functioning vagina or, if preferred, a limited-depth vagina. Either surgery causes the external genitalia to fully appear female. This is by far the most expensive of the transgender surgeries and is less common than you might think. Only 12 percent of the people who participated in the 2015 US Transgender Survey reported having had gender confirmation surgery. (It is important to note, however, that only 62 percent of the survey participants had transitioned publicly.[13])

The female-to-male transition usually begins with medication to stop menstruation, followed by injections of testosterone. Testosterone is a powerful hormone that causes immediate and irreversible changes. Unlike estrogen's inability to alter a voice, testosterone immediately causes the voice to become lower, eventually bringing it within a typical male range. Other changes include skin becoming thicker and rougher, hair becoming coarse, and muscle mass increasing. Fat migrates from hips, thighs, and buttocks to the waist. Facial hair begins to grow, and a more ruddy complexion develops.

Should they choose to undergo surgery, there are three common options for transgender males. The first is a hysterectomy. The second is a double mastectomy. Some choose to also have a phalloplasty, in which a penis is created out of tissue from elsewhere in the body.

As transgender individuals become more accepted by the mainstream population, an increasing number are choosing to forgo surgeries. Only 25 percent of those who responded to the 2015 national survey reported having had any kind of transgender-related surgeries, including gender confirmation surgery as mentioned above.[14] Those who do not choose surgery feel complete in their new gender without it. Others choose to have surgery primarily for the relative safety it affords—transgender people who retain the genitalia of their birth gender are subject to higher levels of violence and greater likelihood of prejudicial treatment.

At the same time, these surgeries don't always lessen the prejudice, discrimination, and danger transgender people experience. Some transgender people have been refused treatment in emergency rooms and medical clinics. Others avoid getting medical treatment because of shame or embarrassment about their bodies. The unfortunate realities of incarceration in America are of particular concern to transgender people. In most jurisdictions, genitalia are the sole determining factor of the gender-specific facility in which an inmate is placed. While surgery can help a transgender person feel more at home in their body, it doesn't always make the world around them a safe or comfortable place to be.

TRANSGENDER CHILDREN AND ADOLESCENTS

People often ask me why we are seeing more and more children identifying as transgender. The truth is that we don't fully understand the reason for this. Are there environmental causes affecting pregnancies and leading to more transgender people? Is the greater acceptance of transgender people making it more likely a person will come out? Is the increased public awareness of transgender people creating a recognition among children that there are more options for gender identity than we knew of in previous generations? We just don't know.

What we do know is that treating children and adolescents who have gender dysphoria is best left to professionals who have experience working with this vulnerable population. Transgender children and adolescents whose parents are not supportive are at high risk for suicide, with a rate far higher than their peers.[15] It is critical that their treatment be of the highest caliber.

Another reason great care should be taken in choosing a therapist for a child who presents as transgender or non-binary is that some children no longer identify as transgender once they become adults. That does not mean being transgender is a choice. It does mean there is more to being transgender than outward appearance or behavior.

An article in the July/August 2018 issue of *The Atlantic* delineates the difference between a child who is clearly transgender and a dysphoric child who is confused about his or her identity and, therefore, may or may not be transgender.[16] Adolescents experience a plethora of fleeting emotions that may or may not be indicators of a deep-seated issue requiring medical intervention. As the public grows more and more accepting of transgender individuals, it is understandable that a child who is feeling uncomfortable in their body might wonder whether or not they have gender dysphoria. That doesn't mean, however, that the child will feel that way in a few months or years. That makes it inadvisable to rush to medical treatments for adolescents who say they are transgender.

The tricky question, of course, is how you determine whether or not a child's claim of gender dysphoria is temporary or is an ongoing and immutable reality. One reliable indicator is the age of onset. A child of three or four who *consistently* and *persistently* claims to be transgender will in all likelihood feel the same as an adult. For that child, an experienced therapist and a physician might begin medical treatment at the age of sixteen, as indicated by WPATH guidelines.

If the first indicators of gender dysphoria don't come until a child is a teenager, more caution is in order. Claiming to be transgender or gender non-binary may, in the extreme, be the actions of a child who is attempting to differentiate from their family of origin in a drastically visible way. While this is highly uncommon and in no way should be used as a dismissal of the experiences of transgender teenagers, it is a possibility and yet another reason why therapy is such a crucial part of a transgender person's coming-out process.

Parents whose children identify as transgender have a number of excellent resources available to them. Organizations like the Trevor Project, PFLAG, GLAAD, the Human Rights Commission, and the Trans Youth Equality Foundation all either specialize in issues related to transgender and non-binary youth, or have significant resources devoted to these children and their families.

THE FAMILY

Cathy and I were the last clients of our marriage therapist on his final day before retirement. I asked, "How many couples are willing to work this hard?" The therapist did not hesitate: "One percent," he said. I asked, "How many get as far as we've gotten?" Again, he didn't hesitate: "One percent. Which is what makes this so tragic. You're a lesbian and your wife is not." That conversation sums up the massive difficulty a family faces when a family member transitions, even when there is deep love and commitment between everyone involved.

I did my best to get through life without transitioning. I did not want my wife and children to suffer. But once I understood I needed to transition, I knew it would be devastating for my family. We are a gendered society, and no one is prepared to hear that their parent or partner or child is not the gender one thought they were.

I am not the one to tell the story of how my family has navigated these difficult waters. That story is theirs to tell. My son, Jonathan, has written a book called She's My Dad *(Westminster John Knox Press).*

It is painful and redemptive, just like the experience of any family determined to stay together through the transition of a family member. I highly recommend it, and not just because he's my son.[17]

When one member of a family transitions, everyone transitions. The entire family narrative is drastically altered, and finding a new normal can take years.

We live in a postmodern environment in which the locus of control for what is understood to be true has shifted. During the first 1,500 years of Western civilization it was the church; for the next 500 years—the Modern Age—it was science. Now the arbiter of what is true has shifted again, to an internal locus of control, with each person determining what is "true for me."

Many people have reacted to this notion by choosing to see only a world in which some kind of external force determines truth. Whether that's a religious body, an ethnic group, a nation-state, a language group, or some other institution, the individual willingly gives his or her unwavering allegiance to that entity and abides by the rules and regulations it has established. While that might provide some modicum of comfort to adherents of that system, it's devastating to friends and family members who fall outside the social norms of that entity.

The transgender population has been caught in the middle of this massive divide. Many on the left celebrate the news that a person has transitioned. They applaud the person's drive to live authentically in their preferred gender. On the other side is a conservative population that has not learned or not embraced the scientific and medical understanding of gender identity and believes it is important to pass laws opposing basic civil rights for transgender people. That leaves few people in the middle, where the family of a transgender person resides. What that family needs is a person who honors the decision of the family member who transitions, while simultaneously honoring the genuine pain experienced by the other members of the family.

A son who feels he has lost his father when his male parent transitions to female might question what it means to be a man. A girl who feels she has lost her mother because her female parent has transitioned might question her own identity. A spouse loses a mate, a partner, a future. Where can those family members go? Resources are slim. Their friends on the left don't understand why the family member can't just celebrate the transition of their loved one. Their friends on the right wonder why they don't reject the transgender family member outright. Neither group provides the kind of deep sensitivity and assistance the family member needs, leaving them to their own resources.

Sensitivity to the family members of transgender people is a good place for advocates to step up and offer care. Recognize that each person in the family will have unique needs—the need to grieve the loss of their parent, the need to begin rebuilding their understanding of what it means to be a family, the need for a safe place to express anger. There will be times when the best support is holding space for the family and times when support means gently encouraging them to move on to the next stage of grieving and living. This is difficult work, but it's an opportunity for faith communities and friends to offer thoughtful, consistent care for a family in the midst of a painful situation.

OFFERING ADVOCACY

Transgender people have no option but to advocate on their own behalf. They need the help of advocates who have no personal stake in working for transgender rights other than the desire to do what is right. We need advocates who will support transgender people in public settings, whether by testifying before legislative bodies; speaking to civic, religious, or educational groups; or talking with friends about what it means to be transgender.

In an age in which misinformation spreads intentionally and quickly, misconceptions about gender dysphoria are rampant. HB-2, the notorious "bathroom bill" in North Carolina that forced transgender individuals to use the restroom corresponding to the gender on their birth certificate, was not based on any empirical evidence. In fact, there is no record of any transgender person ever entering any restroom anywhere for nefarious purposes.

Evangelical Christians were the largest group supporting HB-2, believing their families were at risk. While there is no record of any transgender person being arrested or convicted for entering a restroom to assault others, between 1987 and 2007 the three largest companies that insure Protestant churches paid out 7,095 claims for sexual assault by church leaders, one assault for every twenty-four churches in America. Over 99 percent of the offenders were male.[18] In other words, Americans are exponentially more likely to be sexually assaulted by a male leader in their church than they are to be assaulted by a transgender person.

HB-2 and similar laws are not based on fact. They are based on irrational fear of the "other." The best way to overcome these fears is for people to meet and hear the stories of actual transgender people and make a human connection that dissipates fear.

Unfortunately, such connections are rare—people who are already biased tend not to be willing to place themselves in close proximity to someone who is transgender. (The fact that they interact daily with transgender people without having any idea they are doing so is ironic.) And such interactions ask transgender people to put themselves in potentially dangerous situations where they are at risk of physical and emotional attacks. This is where allies are needed who will speak on behalf of the transgender population, correcting false information and advocating for the basic human rights of transgender people.

CONCLUSION

In the fall of 2017 it was my privilege to speak to 5,200 people at the TEDxMileHigh: Wonder event in Denver, Colorado. That video has been viewed well over 1.5 million times. Below are the words with which I closed that talk. I hope my words provide hope, both for transgender individuals and for their loved ones:

It is hard being a woman. It is hard being a transgender woman. And as a man I just didn't know what I didn't know. Would I do it all again? Of course I would. The call toward authenticity is holy. It is sacred. It is for the greater good.

For forty-five years my father was a fundamentalist pastor. My mother was even more conservative. When I came out as transgender, my parents rejected me. I thought I would never speak to them again. But this past January I called my father on his birthday. He took my call, and we talked for about a half hour. A month later I asked if I could visit, and to my surprise, they said yes.

In April of 2017 I had a delightfully redemptive three-hour visit with my parents. Toward the end of that first visit my father said a number of precious things. As I stood to go, he said, "Paula." That's right, he called me Paula. "Paula, I don't understand this, but I'm willing to try." My father is ninety-three years old, and he is willing to try. What more could I ask? I hugged him so tightly.

One man, giving up his power, because he knew what he knew—that he loved his child—and he would do whatever it takes to honor the journey of another.

Rev. Dr. Paula Stone Williams is the Pastor of Preaching and Worship at Left Hand Church in Longmont, Colorado. She is also the president of RLT Pathways where she provides individual pastoral counseling, ministerial coaching and church consultation. Paula holds a Doctor of Ministry degree in Pastor Care. Paula is on the board of directors of Launch, WITH, and the Q Christian Fellowship. She also serves as a coach for the Center for Progressive Renewal, and is a popular public speaker on issues of gender equality, LGBTQ rights, and current trends in American religion. Paula has been featured in the New York Times, Denver Post, NPR's Radiolab, Radio New Zealand, Colorado Public Radio, the Huffington Post, and TEDxMileHigh.

ENDNOTES

1   *Diagnostic and Statistical Manual of Mental Disorders, Fifth Edition.* American Psychiatric Association (2013): 453.

2   It is less common, though not unheard of, for cross-dressers and drag queens to be female.

3   "How Many Adults Identify as Transgender in the United States," Williams Institute on Sexual Orientation and Gender Identity Law and Public Policy, UCLA School of Law (2016).

4   "Transsexuality Among Twins: Identity Concordance, Transition, Rearing and Orientation," *International Journal of Transgenderism* 14, no. 1 (May 2013).

5   Anne A. Lawrence, "Clinical and Theoretical Parallels between Desire for Limb Amputation and Gender Identity Disorder," *Archives of Sexual Behavior* 35, no. 3 (June 2006): 263–278.

6   "Prevalence of Gender Identity Disorder and Suicide Risk Among Transgender Veterans," *American Journal of Public Health* (October 2013).

7   "Injustice at Every Turn: A Report of the National Transgender Discrimination Survey," National Center for Transgender Equality and National Gay and Lesbian Task Force (2015): 29.

8   Ibid.

9   Arielle Webb et al. "Non-Binary Gender Identities," Society for the Psychological Study of Lesbian, Gay, Bisexual and Transgender Issues, Division 44 of the American Psychological Association (2015).

10   Of course, I am just one transgender person, and the story of one transgender person is just that—the story of one transgender person. I cannot speak for anyone else. There are transgender females who were effeminate as boys, and transgender males who were masculine when they were girls. There are as many different experiences as there are transgender people.

11   "The Report of the US Transgender Survey, 2015," The National Center for Transgender Equality (December 2016).

12   Ibid.

13   Ibid.

14   Ibid.

15   Ibid.

16   Jesse Singal, "Your Child Says She's Trans. She Wants Hormones and Surgery. She's 13," *The Atlantic* (July/August 2018).

17   It was also my son's and my privilege to speak for the TED-Women 2018 event in Palm Springs, California. The video of that presentation, in which we both talked about my transition, is available via YouTube or the TED website.

18   Andrew S. Denney, Kent R. Kerley, Nickolas G. Gross, "Child Sexual Abuse in Protestant Christian Congregations: A Descriptive Analysis of Offense and Offender Characteristics," Department of Criminology and Criminal Justice, University of West Florida (2017).

6

ARE ALL WELCOME?
CREATING AN AUTHENTICALLY AFFIRMING COMMUNITY

BY GEORGE MEKHAIL

Every journey includes milestones that range in significance. Whether a rest stop on the highway, a municipal boundary, or even a historical landmark, milestones help us recall our progression en route to our destination. Sometimes they are planned; other times they are surprises.

In the fall of 2014, I received a text from my close friend Christina that said, "Hey, what are you guys doing right now? We need to talk. Can we come over?"

It was a group text that included my wife, Danielle, and another close friend, Ayla, who also happened to be the nanny to our two kids. At the time, I was the Executive Pastor at EastLake Community Church in Seattle, a unique church that is best known for the story I'm about to share. It was one of the fastest growing non-denominational evangelical mega-churches in the country for several years in a row. At our peak, we hosted more than 5,000 people each Sunday, and around the time I got the text from

Christina, we were meeting across seven different locations in the Seattle area. Christina was on staff as a music/worship leader, and Ayla was part of EastLake's internship program, which I was leading at the time. It was a Saturday night, which meant three of us had to be at work very early the next morning. I didn't realize it at the time, but this detail would go on to shape how I view the conversations around sexuality in the church. This night became a landmark in my life as a pastor.

Let me give you a little background. At this point in EastLake's story, our lead pastor, Ryan Meeks, the rest of our leadership team, and I had been deep into conversations about becoming an open and affirming church. The questions we were wrestling with had hovered within the hypothetical and theological realms for quite some time. We'd talk about the various nuances of sexuality, including a brief exploration of whether it made sense for us to become a "Side B" church, which meant "allowing" LGBTQ Christians to be out, as long as they remained celibate. We navigated questions around the nuances of language and the difference between calling ourselves "welcoming" vs. "accepting" vs. "affirming." The conversations were typically stressful because we were essentially challenging each other to rethink our entire worldview—most of us had grown up with meaningless messages like "Homosexuality is a sin," and while we'd all backed away from that ideology, it was still lingering in each of us in distinct ways that made finding agreement a fraught process.

Despite our slow roll-out on the public-facing side of the decision to be an open and affirming church, our entire staff had spent many months navigating those behind-the-scenes conversations I mentioned above. The practical implications were typically an afterthought, and these discussions hadn't yet been made public in any official capacity. Still, if you had been around our church, you could likely sense that change was imminent—or at the very least, you might wonder if we were still an evangelical church. We had begun incorporating liturgical elements into our services that were often deemed "too traditional" for our crowd. When we decided we were going to offer communion every Sunday and provide stations for people to light candles, there were complaints that we were becoming too "new age-y." If that makes zero sense to you, you're in good company! Entire staff meetings were dedicated to our evolving thought process. We read and studied books on LGBTQ inclusion and were committed to being the church we knew we needed to be. We understood that the only thing left for us to do as a church was to actually make a formal announcement. At least, that's what I thought until Christina and Ayla showed up at our house.

Danielle, Christina, Ayla, and I settled in. I could tell our friends had something on their minds—this was a late-night, last-minute get-together and it felt significant. And it was.

The conversation went something like this:

Me: So . . . what's going on?
Christina: Well . . . I like Ayla.
Me [smiling]: And does Ayla feel the same about you?
Ayla [laughs]: Yes, of course!
Me: Yay! That's fantastic news. Congrats!

Danielle and I jumped off the couch, hugged them both, and beamed at the blooming young love they had just shared with us. We were genuinely happy for our friends. This was the easy part, full of authentic joy, laughter, and excitement. (I shudder to think about how this interaction would have gone if I had still believed the conservative theology I had embraced until about a year before this conversation.)

These two had many more emotionally exhausting conversations ahead, and I imagine it was a relief once Danielle and I were in the loop. But something still seemed unresolved—there was more they still hadn't shared. Our mini-celebration gave way to the palpable tension that had inspired this impromptu meeting in the first place. I leaned in:

Me: So, how can we be most supportive?
Christina: [struggling for words]

Ayla: She thinks you're going to fire her.
Christina [through tears]: Am I still going to be able to lead worship tomorrow?

I was speechless. Why would she question our acceptance of her? I passionately dismissed any notion that her status at EastLake would change, laughing off the idea that she would now be disqualified. My attempts to deliver comfort and reassurance seemed helpful at the time, but the reality we all understood was that my *personal* decision to embrace their love without hesitation was just that: my personal decision. Although I had confidence it would all be okay, Christina's uncertainty caught me off guard. At the very least, I wasn't the final authority on the matter, which meant it was still unclear, even to me, how things would play out at a newly progressive, non-denominational, evangelical, multi-site mega-church once the conversation about LGBTQ inclusion officially ceased to be hypothetical. There were real-world implications for the queer people who had been hurt by the Christian community in the past and were rightly hesitant to let their guard down. Two of those people were sitting right in front of me.

As more and more churches and denominations become welcoming and inclusive to LGBTQ people, there remain real questions about inclusion that even progressive churches need to wrestle with. It's easy to wave a rainbow flag outside your church building and say all the correct words about being open and affirming. But often, our good intentions and desire to create a welcoming environment are overly optimistic—not to mention simplistic—and cause us to neglect defining and communicating the practical details and structural implications of inclusion. That leaves the LGBTQ people who show up or come out or point out that they've been in our communities all along guessing what this means for them. Are they invited into some parts of the community but not others— not leadership, for example? Is their presence and involvement truly welcome or simply tolerated? Are they held to the same expectations about relationships, marriage, and parenting as straight and cisgender people in the congregation, or is there a separate set of assumptions? When churches don't clarify these questions from the beginning, they put the safety and well-being of LGBTQ people at risk.

As church leaders in the twenty-first century, our strategic focus is largely tainted by an ingrained scarcity mentality. This causes us to approach decisions around inclusion primarily through a lens of what we might lose, rather than asking what the right next step might be. We focus on questions about how many big givers will bail or how long it will take to run out of money if we are too bold or come across as radical in our policies and practices. I've seen this play out in many local church communities where the pastor holds very different theological convictions about sexuality than the congregation. Rather than live into their convictions, these pastors are paralyzed by fear and seduced by comfort.

I've personally known pastors who have actually just quit ministry as a result of this pressure, choosing to step away rather than take a stand. You may remember the case of World Vision, a global evangelical organization that caused a stir in 2014 when its CEO announced they would hire LGBTQ people, including those who were in same-sex marriages. After two days of intense pressure from the evangelical community, the company reversed its decision, devastating those who had seen the initial announcement as a sign of hope and inclusion. I've often wondered how much this situation caused other religious organizations to become even further entrenched and fearful about moving toward welcome for LGBTQ people.

As I look back to that evening at our house, I feel some relief that my personal response was genuinely loving. But Christina's question hit me hard that night, and it still haunts me. EastLake was extremely well suited to undergo the theological transformation of becoming open and affirming, primarily because we had a lead pastor who was humble, curious, and largely supported in his personal spiritual journey by our leadership team, staff, and congregation. But despite the relationships our pastors and leadership team had cultivated and the thoughtfulness we assumed we'd invested into the process, Christina's question exposed *structural* deficiencies that we had yet to address.

As it turned out, we had been distracted by the nebulous goal of "bringing people along," rather than addressing practical concerns the queer person might be wondering about, like, "Am I still going to be able to lead worship tomorrow?" The allure of meaningless, circular, theoretical debates was more exciting. We'd read all of our progressive Christian heroes and felt equipped to navigate questions about the so-called "clobber verses" in the Bible that are used to deny inclusion to LGBTQ people in the church. We were prepared to do battle with the "Wikipedia theologians" who have read just enough to suddenly begin monopolizing our post-sermon receiving lines, email inboxes, and social media mentions. But we weren't quite ready to admit that we were already undermining our efforts to cultivate an inclusive community by not thinking through the actual church experience of LGBTQ people.

While EastLake is not a cautionary tale, we learned a great deal, especially from people like Christina and Ayla, who continued their trailblazing journey with incredible courage and vulnerability. They essentially carried our leadership team across the finish line to becoming a fully inclusive church. We didn't do everything right, and there are certainly things we'd do differently, but we learned a handful of lessons that are valuable and applicable to any church seeking to go beyond good intentions and token expressions of acceptance for LGBTQ people.

KNOW WHO'S DOING THIS WELL

One of the first lessons we learned as we started in on the work of being an inclusive community was that we were at least thirty years behind the mainline church. If you're in the mainline church, you might be thinking, "Yeah, you were." But I can't overstate how eye-opening it was for me, a twenty-nine-year-old former Calvinist, to discover that a) There were churches outside of the evangelical orbit I'd been in, and b) They had broken ground on inclusion before I was even born. It was stunning news for me—and a few of my fellow staff members—to realize we had something to learn from those "old-fashioned" churches.

Even if your church is already an inclusive congregation, it's worth looking at other institutions and organizations that have been doing reconciliation work in areas such as race or gender to see how they communicate their stance to the public and to their membership. It's also important to keep in mind how rapidly things are evolving around this topic and how momentum works. When the pioneers of mainline Protestant denominations took on the imperative of inclusion more than three decades ago, they were so far ahead of the movement that they found limited solidarity. These trailblazers were never even allowed to penetrate the more conservative factions of the church with their message of love and inclusion.

Things are different now. Standing on the shoulders of those who have gone before us, a handful of churches from every corner of the faith have been building a new wave of momentum that is already altering the landscape of inclusion. A cursory internet search reveals a number of movements that continue to grow in influence, which is encouraging for anyone wrestling with their next steps.

FOCUS ON THE PEOPLE WHO STAY

In the midst of our long discernment process, we brought pastor and author Brian McLaren out to preach and spend time with our staff. I'll never forget his advice as we wrestled with our next steps: "Focus on the people who stay. Focus on the people who stay. Focus on the people who stay." Simple wisdom for effectiveness, repeated by a wise sage with conviction that rendered the prevailing "bring people along" strategy utterly foolish.

We had previously penciled in an announcement about becoming open and affirming several months into the future. We thought we needed to lay some groundwork in an attempt to get people more comfortable with the idea, so we had planned a sermon series about love and relationships. But after meeting with Brian, we realized it was impossible to pretend we weren't making this change, and pointless to try to ease people into something that was going to happen whether they were ready for it or not.

That meant pushing past a lot of fear. Fear is an incredibly powerful motivator that causes us to do things we otherwise wouldn't, or to not do things we'd otherwise have no problem doing. Perhaps fear's most misleading quality is how it distorts reality, conceals its spell over us, and convinces us that we've actually conquered the thing we were originally afraid of. But fear has extra lives—even when we think we've killed it, it comes back in a different, more insidious form. This is particularly true when you happen to be making a complete 180-degree turn from the faith you grew up with and everything you believe about God. With each step we took, fear assured us we had done enough: Just thinking about calling ourselves open and affirming made us more progressive than any of our peers. We were heretics by now in many circles. We had arrived at a familiar paradigm where we were convinced we believed "correctly." The further along on the journey we were, the more self-assured fear made us, falsely confirming that our demons had been conquered. Each "progressive" step we took was scary because we knew it meant losing people, losing money, and, at some level, adding to our existential dread about life and death and salvation and all of that. But fear told us we were kicking its ass. We were not.

Equipped with McLaren's wisdom, we began paying closer attention to the different ways people approached us and calibrating our responses accordingly. We slowly stopped arguing theology with those who hinted at leaving if we made this decision. We dropped the pretense of engaging with those who clearly wanted to argue with us for sport, and focused on thoughtful conversations with people who sincerely wanted to learn more. The re-centering of people who wanted to stay was incredibly freeing. It allowed us to remain realistic about the implications of inclusion—we would lose people—while providing us a critical opportunity to re-examine our fear-based motivations—we didn't have to be afraid of losing people. This meant we could actually start thinking about the future, rather than remaining trapped in a pattern of self-preservation. We exchanged notes among our team and noticed a lightness and relief in our newfound approach.

FOCUS ON POLICY, NOT POSTURING

Belief is cute. It allows us to construct entire worlds on its vast terrain of unlimited hypotheticals. The problem with belief when you are a church leader attempting to cultivate a more inclusive environment within the well-worn confines of a community is that belief doesn't do very much. It's like that episode of *The Office* where Michael Scott walks in and screams, "I declare bankruptcy!"—as if that's all there was to the process. This is what we were doing—declaring something ("We're super progressive!") without really changing anything. It's what many churches do when it comes to inclusion—of LGBTQ people, of women, of people of color, of any group or anything that might pull us off script and into uncomfortable places of change.

Just ask Christina. All those conversations about how inclusive we were, all the books we were reading, all the progressive churches we were visiting were fantastic. But inclusion isn't contagious. Being around it or intellectually agreeing to an inclusive worldview doesn't do anything until it is manifested in the most unsexy way imaginable: actively enforced policy.

Every church (and organization, for that matter) has policies that it actively enforces. This is the fundamental nature of being an organization. Even if it's a policy that's rarely enforced, or a policy the leaders of the organization don't personally agree with, policy is the institutional outworking of belief. At EastLake, the first "policy" we enforced that crystalized our new beliefs into concrete action was when we easily and unanimously formalized the decision to not fire Christina. It also exposed the thickest layer of fear we had managed to avoid so far: Would we make formal policies to promote inclusion? We finally did kick fear to the curb by publicly declaring our decision to change our policies to formally include our LGBTQ siblings in full participation at every level of the EastLake community.

REPENTANCE 101

Flying a rainbow flag doesn't mean anything if there are no actively enforced policies to go with it. Each church needs to decide for itself what those policies will be, but they simply must be in place—and taken seriously—if a church is going to call itself welcoming, affirming, inclusive, or open to LGBTQ people.

After years of intense conversation, soul searching, and planning, we arrived at the Sunday when Ryan was going to announce EastLake as an open and affirming church. All seven of our locations heard a sermon that was unapologetic and rich with conviction. The only apology in the sermon was reserved for the LGBTQ community, for the harm the church had inflicted historically and for taking so long to come to this realization. This was an important and healing step that can get overlooked in conversations about churches becoming inclusive. Church leaders who are committed to radical justice don't get a pass for prior behavior that was problematic. Of course, we know that—we're pastors. Repentance requires us to do everything in our power to make amends and, indeed, reparations for our previously misguided ways.

"Saying sorry" is often a great place to start, but it's also only meaningful if you actually move beyond lip service. The sermon's most powerful moment was when Ryan read our formal statement of inclusion, openly stating the changes in policy and moving us beyond hypothetical inclusion. At the time, EastLake was one of the largest evangelical churches to publicly become affirming. All this really means is that we likely hold a record for Fastest Drop in Church Attendance in modern history.

LET YOUR YES BE YES

It didn't take long to hear from pastors from all over the world. As you can probably imagine, we received several categories of feedback: shock, excitement, anger, fear, and insecurity. I remember one particular instance when a pastor sheepishly approached me and a few of my colleagues at a conference. He looked around nervously to make sure no one was watching, then said, "Please don't say anything because I would lose my job, but I'm really excited about what you're doing at EastLake. Keep up the good work!" Then—*poof!*—he vanished into the crowd, never to so much as make eye contact with us for the rest of the conference.

These types of interactions happened more than I had expected, to the point where it was difficult to ignore or dismiss it as anything other than endemic. Observing the behavior of church leaders who expressed support privately, but not so much publicly, is one of the most instructive dynamics for understanding the dysfunctional symptoms plaguing the church. On one hand, I get it. People are stressed out about what will happen to their churches if they shake things up. Even in mainline churches whose denominations have made statements about inclusion, there can be resistance to full inclusion because a handful of people will make a fuss about it, or it's just too much work, or it involves rewriting bylaws. On the other hand, I don't have much patience with this particular condition. By not asking simple questions about the communities we are a part of, we perpetuate harmful structures in the name of preserving our own comfort. No one benefits from this.

RESIST EVANGELISM

For several months after EastLake's announcement and the subsequent operational crisis mode our church was in, we ran on the passion of our scrappy little community. We lost nearly 2,500 people in the first year, and our annual budget dropped by about $4 million—roughly half on both counts. Yes, it was terrifying to our material sensibilities, but it was exhilarating to be free to be the church we knew we needed to be. I was convinced that the next season of ministry would be fruitful—we'd crossed the Rubicon of evangelicalism and God hadn't struck us with lightning! Surely this meant credibility and perhaps a revival throughout our substantial network of evangelical pastors! We would shout our story from the rooftops, sharing it with anyone who would listen! Perhaps they would see the light and follow us down the path of inclusion! Helping churches become affirming was my new Great Commission. And for a few short months, these were my self-appointed marching orders.

It didn't take long for me to realize this was an unhealthy and unrealistic posture. The conversations I had with previously supportive pastors were becoming increasingly awkward, if not downright contentious. The topic of LGBTQ inclusion began dominating every interaction with pastor friends and Christian leaders, often with confrontation being the only real goal for either side. After a while, the arguments I heard against inclusion became predictable and lazy. Hearing the same four talking points week in and week out made it clear to me that people weren't actually listening. They didn't want to know how to create welcoming communities. They just wanted me to defend our decision to be such a place. What began as an energetic desire to be helpful eventually became counterproductive, often leaving me frustrated and feeling hopeless about the church and my place in it.

There's a tendency among churches that make big changes like this to hold ourselves in high esteem, to see ourselves as exemplars of bold leadership and theological progress. And whether we are overtly evangelistic about it or simply lord it over churches that haven't followed our lead, this sense of pride in our progressiveness can easily derail the good intentions behind it. Being a welcoming, inclusive church isn't a badge of honor. It's an act of justice. It's the bare minimum.

One of my all-time favorite YouTube videos is of a cute toddler working on unbuckling a car seat. The child's dad offers help, but the toddler politely declines and goes on to tell the dad, "Worry 'bout yourself." If you haven't seen it, I would highly encourage you to pause here and spend the ninety seconds to take a look. I'll wait.

Despite the child's obvious struggles to release the lock on the seatbelt, the child wants to take care of it alone. This is a child making steps toward independence and self-sufficiency, and will ask for help when they're ready. We are not responsible for other people's journeys toward inclusion for LGBTQ people or any other theological position. Whether it's the church down the road or parishioners who are resistant to change, we have to let other people unlock themselves in their own time.

I had to ask myself why I felt the need to convert people in the first place. Was it really about justice and standing up for the most marginalized (like I told myself), or was it actually just a repackaged version of certainty I'd held in my early faith journey? Many progressive Christians, often former evangelicals like me, get stuck in this mode. Rather than fully embodying the freedom that comes with a more inclusive theology, we revert to old habits and insist that others adopt our worldview. Progressive legalism is still legalism. Releasing my need to change someone's theology is the single most freeing worldview shift I've made, probably in my entire life. I'm resisting the temptation now to try to get you to agree with that, so we'll leave it there.

SEEK CLARITY

As much as I believe "Worry 'bout yourself" is an excellent theological posture, it doesn't address the ambiguity that Christina felt so acutely. I could be okay with leaving pastors to their own devices and accepting their desire to remain non-affirming—there was more than enough work to do in our own setting—but I was not okay with the pattern of harmful ambiguity I saw in churches. I realized that vague rhetoric on websites and from the pulpit espousing inclusive language despite non-affirming policies is often just as harmful to LGBTQ people as outright exclusion. Gradually, I shifted my conversations with other leaders so the goal was clarity, not conversion.

I started to ask other pastors to clarify their church's position on LGBTQ inclusion. I was stunned to discover that this opened up far different conversations than my previous efforts to get people on the same page as me. People who disagreed with me theologically actually agreed that pastors and churches should be clear about their position and their actively enforced policies, that this is the loving and compassionate thing to do. I would argue that it's more loving to be non-affirming and to be clear about that than to pretend to be affirming or to mislead people about the extent to which your policies reflect authentic inclusion for all. So many LGBTQ people have been wounded over and over again by churches that refuse to do the real work involved in making themselves a welcoming, inclusive community.

Clarity comes when churches can match up their beliefs and their policies. I caution leaders about assuming they are automatically aligned, or that bringing the two into alignment is easy. There is real work involved in making your church an inclusive community. And everyone in the church needs to know where it stands. Avoiding that work or assuming you've done it without genuine evaluation opens the church up for doing real harm to people—people like my friend, who was part of a church where the pastor told him emphatically that he was supported and would officiate at the wedding "no matter which gender" he married. But when he became engaged to a man, the pastor backtracked, telling my friend there was too much pressure from the big donors and he just couldn't risk alienating them by officiating at this wedding. A clear policy, even one that said the church would not perform same-sex weddings, would have spared my friend this tremendous betrayal at the hands of a well-meaning, but ultimately misleading church.

Look at the policies already in place in your church. Are there any that are out of sync with your beliefs? Any that hamstring your vision for the kind of church you want to be? Make sure your church website goes beyond platitudes like "All are welcome" and explicitly states that there are no limitations on LGBTQ people within your community. Amplify these policies so the whole church knows them—even your big donors. Implore your denomination to do the same. The LGBTQ pride flag is a fine gesture, but there is simply no substitute for a clearly defined, easily accessible, and actively enforced policy.

LGBTQ affirmation is just the tip of the iceberg. The truth is, churches are ambiguous on a lot of their policies. Can women preach? Can a woman be senior pastor? Will the church hire a pastor who is trans? How do these decisions even get made? The answers to these questions have significant influence on shaping a community. I'm certainly not the one to tell you how your church should answer them. But I will say that the only way to create communities of faith where people are genuinely welcome, where everyone knows where they stand, is to create and communicate clear policies that perfectly mirror the stated beliefs of the church. Openness and affirmation are just words until they are backed up with real structural change. At the end of the day, this is a gospel issue (as we like to say in the biz), which is to say it's a matter of justice. To persist in a state of ambiguity is to avoid truth. Evading the truth by ignoring our structural deficiencies makes us prisoners of our own sterilized comfort, while embracing the truth sets us free.

George Mekhail is the executive director and architect of Church Clarity, a social impact organization focused on establishing a new standard of clarity for protestant churches. He and his family are bi-coastal, living in Seattle suburbs and Brooklyn, NY, attempting to chase down as many dreams as possible. George has been in church leadership since 2011; prior to that he spent eight years in the Real Estate industry. George is a leader, pastor, writer, dreamer, activist, husband, and father.

7

BUILDING AN ETHIC OF SEXUAL WHOLENESS

SEEKING A NEW WAY FORWARD

BY REV. MARCUS G. HALLEY

I don't remember my parents ever having "the talk" with me. That doesn't necessarily mean "the talk" never happened. It means that, if it did, it was either so incredibly awkward or so incredibly unhelpful that I simply don't remember it. In fact, I don't remember sex ever being talked about positively in my family, if at all, which was unfortunate because it was all over the television and every other popular form of media.

My church, on the other hand, didn't shy away from talking about sex. It was easy to assume from the way my childhood church engaged scripture that Jesus' primary concerns were, in this order: sex, tithing, and amassing blessings like young me collecting limited-edition Pokémon cards. When the conversation did turn to sex, it was often reductionistic, unhelpful, and shaming. I later came to see that this was not unique to my church but was common across many Christian communities. So often, sex is framed as a constant taboo that only finds a modicum of holiness within the context of a heterosexual marriage. Any other kind of sex is to be avoided at all costs. The message of my youth was that our bodies are simultaneously "temples of the Holy Spirit" and dens of iniquity, a contradiction that made it difficult to embrace a narrative of positive embodiment—the idea that living in our bodies was a good and holy thing.

The way sex was talked about in my family and in my church had one thing in common—shame. Shame silenced my parents and prevented my church from engaging in conversations around sex from a perspective of fullness, hope, intimacy, and resiliency. This shame was deposited in me as well. Having to grow up in both a family and a church that struggled to talk about sex, I was unable to find safe places to talk about my own developing sexuality. Everything I came to know about sex and sexuality I had to discover from other resources or through trial and error.

The conversation around sex, particularly in faith communities or families for whom faith is an important source of guidance, is often cloaked in this shame. If it is addressed at all, the topic of sex is handled in such a way as to ignore our embodied spirits and instead focus exclusively on genitals and biology. These conversations ignore the deeper ethical, emotional, and spiritual questions people have about sex and sexuality, leaving most of us to our own flawed and furtive investigations.

I also believe this represents a massive misunderstanding of sexuality. I'm aware that there has often been a reticence to engage in the conversation of sexuality from a theological framework because our access to theological resources on sexuality has been truncated by shame. It is also true that too often, when theology has been applied to sexuality, it has been benignly unhelpful or openly hostile and dangerous to certain bodies, particularly female, transgender, or queer bodies. This can be seen in the amount of time religious conversations on sexuality devote to policing the bodies of women and the behavior of non-straight people instead of helping each of us feel at home in our own bodies.

In order to develop a narrative that supports us, provides a helpful theological framework for sex and sexuality, and advocates for the protection of certain bodies, we must broaden our theological scope and chart new waters. For this, we turn to Jesus, who was kind of amazing at charting new spiritual waters.

In Luke's Gospel, Jesus is asked to arbitrate a legal matter between two brothers. As he responds to their conflict, Jesus orients his followers toward the signs of God's reign on earth and away from trivial matters like amassing wealth. Then he says something that I want to explore as a point of departure toward a faithful practice of sexual wholeness: "Do not worry about your life, what you will eat, or about your body, what you will wear," Jesus says. "For life is more than food, and the body more than clothing" (Luke 12:22-23). At face value, this has little to do with sex and sexuality; however, the rest of Jesus' response suggests that God is deeply invested in the well-being of our bodies. "Consider the lilies, how they grow . . . if God so clothes the grass of the field . . . how much more will he clothe you?" (Luke 12:27-28). Jesus seems to suggest that God cares about our bodies—they are a high priority for God—and that our bodies are worth more than what we put on them or into them. They have an inherent value and that impacts how we live in them, what we do with them, and how we view and engage our bodies and the bodies of others. God cares about more than our spirits. God is concerned about who we are as a unified being. God cares about our whole selves.

What follows is my attempt to explore sex and sexuality from a theological framework of wholeness. It's my belief that sex is good, that our sexuality is both a gift from and a way of experiencing the divine, and that our bodies are blessings. We'll start with my own story and what I've discovered and learned about sex and sexuality, before dipping into the well of Christian tradition for wisdom that support human flourishing in particular bodies, and finally ending up with an exploration of what sexual wholeness might look like as a practice. Because both sex and sexuality are messy, complex, and highly nuanced, my hope is not to offer answers, but to draw the landscape of sexuality in the context of our faith tradition so that individuals can live out a sexual ethic that reunites body and soul—both considered integral—in one beloved creation of God.

A TRADITION OF AMBIVALENCE

One of the first stops we need to make in order to embrace a positive Christian ethic of sexual wholeness is to take a look at the Bible. It might come as a surprise that Christianity seems ambivalent about sex and sexuality. There are some passages of the Bible that seem to embrace sex and sexuality as positive, while others treat it either as a necessary evil to be tepidly embraced or something to be actively avoided altogether.

The most obvious example of sex-positivity in the Bible is the Song of Solomon (or the Song of Songs), where sex and sexuality are held in high regard. While early Christian writers and theologians understood this writing as an allegory of the love between God and Israel—and later an allegory of the love between Christ and his church—when read at face value, this writing describes and celebrates love and intimacy between two human beings with sufficient sexual imagery to make the average churchgoer blush.

Other places in the Bible frame sex as something to be avoided. The apostle Paul, who was unmarried during his work as a missionary, tells the Corinthian church, "I wish that all were as I myself am" (1 Corinthians 7:7). Prior to that, he concedes that sex is a reality, but should only happen within the context of a marriage wherein "the husband should give to his wife her conjugal rights, and likewise the wife to her husband" (1 Corinthians 7:3). While his exploration of marriage here can be praised for its egalitarian quality—which would have been something of a novelty during the time period—it's clear that Paul doesn't speak of sex as a joy, but as a duty. He almost suggests that sex is something to be tolerated as a part of a relationship, not embraced and celebrated. Not exactly worthy of a Hallmark card.

Other areas in the Bible describe sex in incredibly problematic terms. There are many places in Scripture where rape and sexual violence occur and, at least according to the writers, these incidents are either ignored or condoned by God. Other times, sexuality, particularly female sexuality, is used as a negative trope to describe the dysfunctional relationship between God and God's people. Examples of this include the sexual slavery of Hagar (Genesis 16) and Bilhah and Zilpah (Genesis 30), the relationship between Hosea and Gomer as an allegory of the disobedience of the Israelites toward God ("Please with your mother, plead—for she is not my wife and I am not her husband—that she put away her whoring from her face" [Hosea 2:2]), and references to the "great whore" in the book of Revelation. These negative portrayals of female sexuality are worthy of critique, particularly in the age of the #MeToo and #ChurchToo movements when many women (and supportive men) are calling out the abuse of the power provided to men by a patriarchal system. Using these passages of Scripture to construct an ethic of sexual wholeness requires that sexual violence and abuse of any kind be denounced; that the experiences of victims be raised up and heard, believed, and healed; and that the perpetrators of such violence—as well as the systems and cultures that condoned the behavior—be critiqued and corrected.

It also requires us to amplify female voices within Scripture, even and especially when those voices are not present in stories even thought their bodies are. Wil Gafney's *Womanist Midrash* raises up the voices of women in the Hebrew Bible quite well, engaging the midrashic tradition of Hebrew scripture to grant female characters in the Bible more complete stories.[1] (If you don't know what *midrash* is, think biblical fan fiction that fills in the gaps of the original story. It's pretty amazing!) Gafney humanizes the women, which is crucial. Too often, the church has interpreted women's sexuality without including women's voices, either physically keeping women from rooms of power or rhetorically erasing them from their own stores. When, for example, Gafney grants Hagar a full story, including her death in Egypt, she recovers a lost narrative. We are given a more fully human Hagar, a person in her own right who is not defined by her proximity to men.

The Bible's ambivalence to sex and sexuality continues into and through Christian history. Take the writings of St. Augustine of Hippo and St. Hildegard of Bingen, for example. In his *Confessions,* St. Augustine writes extensively of his struggle against sexual desire, calling it a "disordered" desire:

All these things are the gift of my God: I did not give them to myself. These things are good, and they all made up my being. Therefore, he who made me is good, and he is my good ... But in this was my sin, that not in him but in his creatures, in myself and others, did I seek pleasure, honors, and truths.[2]

On the other hand, St. Hildegard, in addition to her writings on her own mystical experiences, recorded one of the world's earliest known descriptions of the female orgasm from a female perspective. It's clear that, even as a celibate nun, she believed sexuality and divinity were not mutually exclusive, but two sides of one coin, the coin being our selves. In her *Causae at Curae* she writes:

When a woman is making love with a man, a sense of heat in her brain, which brings with it sensual delight, communicates the taste of that delight during the act and summons forth the emission of the man's seed. And when the seed has fallen into its place, that vehement heat descending from her brain draws the seed to itself and holds it, and soon the woman's sexual organs contract, and all the parts that are ready to open up during the time of menstruation now close, in the same way as a strong man can hold something enclosed in his fist.[3]

Yes, a nun wrote that.

What each of these sources point out is the variety of voices speaking about sex from a spiritual and theological background. They also point out the pitfalls that open when this subject is approached too narrowly. When the church distills this rich and

layered conversation into neat boxes marked "right" and "wrong,"
"yes" and "no," it usually has negative implications for female, queer,
and trans people, automatically dismissing and even vilifying their
experiences. Embracing the wide array of voices and experiences in
our tradition might be a step in the right direction.

HOLY DESIRE

As we have seen, the Bible and Christian tradition are not of one
mind when it comes to sex and sexuality, so any narrative of sexual
wholeness must be willing to ask the questions people actually
think about. Instead of seeking hard-and-fast rules, I often wonder
if conversations about sex and sexuality in the church ought to
aim at developing wisdom about our bodies, helping us understand
and know "not only what is true of our bodies, but also when it's
true,"[4] to borrow a phrase from Rachel Held Evans. Rather than
approaching our Christian tradition to ask whether something is
right or wrong, maybe we need to be asking if something is just
or unjust. Am I honoring my body and depth of my desire? Am I
honoring the body and depth of desire of another?

In 1989 address, Rowan Williams, former Archbishop of Canterbury,
gave an address to the Lesbian and Gay Christian Movement called,
"The Body's Grace." In his words, "The whole story of creation,
incarnation and our incorporation into the fellowship of Christ's
body tells us that God desires us, as if we were God, as if we were
that unconditional response to God's giving that God's self makes
in the life of the trinity."[5] Here's what he's getting at: For Williams,
because we are creatures of God and objects of God's desire, our
human desire is merely an extension of God's, meant to complete
the circle of creation—God desires us, God's desire lives in us, and
we extend that desire back to God. The Incarnation, the moment in
which the infinite God of the universe became finite and human, is
an example of the degree of God's desire for us.

If we're going to build a positive ethic of sexual wholeness, we
have to have a positive understanding of desire in general. In an

essay entitled "Use of the Erotic," author Audre Lorde expounds upon the nature of desire with beautiful depth. Stick with me here. Remember, conversations around sex and sexuality are often reduced to meaningless platitudes—we've lost some language for talking about them—so we think of eroticism as meaning something like "lust," which is routinely denounced in the Bible. But Lorde suggests that eroticism is deeper than mere lust. She writes:

> The erotic functions for me in several ways, and the first is in providing the power which comes from sharing deeply any pursuit with another person. The sharing of joy, whether physical, emotional, psychic, or intellectual, forms a bridge between the sharers which can be the basis for understanding much of what is not shared between them, and lessens the threat of their difference.[6]

Rather than reducing desire to objectifying another person, Lorde frames it as something that helps us move beyond our fears and connects us to one another. In other words, desire is deeply humanizing.

Picking up on this theme of desire as crossing vast chasms of difference, Rowan Williams suggests that "grace, for the Christian believer, is a transformation that depends in large part on knowing yourself to be seen in a certain way: as significant, as wanted."[7] We experience God's grace because God desires us, and as a result, God, in Jesus, bridges the chasm of difference between Creator and creature so that we can know God and God's grace. What a gift! God desires us so much that God fills the space between us in order to draw us closer.

It's the work of the Christian community, then, to teach us how to have the kind of relationships in which "human beings may see themselves as *desired.*"[8] While desire is often cast in purely or primarily sexual terms, both Lorde and Williams choose to use it as a way of speaking to something deep within the human condition—the need to be affirmed, seen, and celebrated.

Remember Augustine and his disordered desire? For Augustine, desire originates from and finds its proper home in God but becomes disordered in human beings. He writes:

> The good you love is from [God], but only in so far as it is used for him is it good and sweet. But with justice will it become bitter, if you, as a deserter from him, unjustly love what comes from him. Whither do you walk, farther and farther along these hard and toilsome roads? There is no rest to be found where you seek it: seek what you seek, but it lies not where you seek it. You seek a happy life in the land of death, but it is not there. How can you find a happy life where there is no life?[9]

Augustine is basically saying that the desire we have from God can only be fulfilled in God. Outside of God, desire is only a shadow of what it could be. It's unfortunate that Augustine's words lack a positive understanding of this incarnation or embodiment. He only offers the negative—that searching for fulfillment anywhere but in God alone will lead to heartache and disappointment. That doesn't leave much room for human interaction.

Here's where I feel like I should give a little grace to St. Augustine. I affirm both his deep sense of longing, and his belief that our ultimate desire is to be found in God and God alone. I also want to affirm something Augustine seems reluctant to: that we can be fulfilled, albeit to a lesser degree than in God, in our relationships with one another. If incarnation matters and if God is concerned about the lilies, then our bodies are important here. This brings us back to what Williams suggests, that the central work of the church is to teach us to understand and create our relationships with one another through the lens of the gospel so that we can see and experience ourselves as desired of God.

AT HOME IN THE BODY

A positive ethic of Christian sexual wholeness affirms this deep human need for connection by seeing sexuality as a manifestation of that need. We need to be affirmed, seen, and celebrated by those we desire. This is why sex is risky. In the experience of sex, we are incredibly vulnerable—naked, seen for who we are, and touched deeply and intimately. Perhaps this explains the passion around sex and sexuality, particularly in the context of the contemporary American church. Sex is a big deal, and it connects to a deep part of who we are and how we exist in the world. Understanding it as an expression of a broader desire can help us better understand what we are truly yearning for beyond the biological needs satisfied by sex.

In addition, affirming incarnation as an expression of the goodness of our bodies is crucial to building a positive ethic of Christian sexual wholeness. God sees our bodies as so good and worthy of celebration and honor that God chose to physically inhabit one such body. This also shows up in Paul's letters. When choosing a metaphor to describe the early Christian community, Paul chooses the body. He writes, "For just as the body is one and has many members, and all the members of the body, though many, are one body, so it is with Christ" (1 Corinthians 12:12). This is surprising coming from the same apostle who bemoaned his embodiment in his letter to the Romans (Romans 7:24). Not only does this point to the complexity of our experience as embodied beings, but, it also points out the ability to draw grace from the experience of being human. If bodies are good enough to house divinity and to be used as allegories of the mystical connection between God's people, then bodies must be good.

In her book, *Honoring the Body: Meditations on a Christian Practice,* theologian Stephanie Paulsell suggests that:

> The affirmation that every body is made in the image of God is supplemented in Christianity by the belief that God was somehow fully present in a particular human body that lived in a particular time and place, the body of Jesus of Nazareth. The Church has used the word *incarnation* to describe the conviction that God was *in-carnate,* enfleshed in a body that ate and drank, slept and worked, touched and received touch.

This body also suffered a death as painful and degrading as any human beings have devised. Early Christian testimony that this body also lived again after death shapes a profound Christian hope that undergirds the practice of honoring the body. Whatever else it means, the Resurrection of Jesus suggests that bodies matter to God. And they ought to matter to us too.[10]

Our bodies are not liabilities to God; they are assets. They are tools, residences for the divine, even temples of the Holy Spirit. Any Christian conversation of our bodies must include this concept of positive embodiment or else it proves both unfaithful and unhelpful. Positive embodiment is a necessary piece off a positive ethic of Christian sexual wholeness. As the writer of the Acts of Apostles suggests, what God has called good we must not call evil (Acts 10:15).

Paulsell also explores all the ways Christianity calls us to honor the human body, even going so far as to call to our attention the sacred nature of mundane practices like eating, rest, and dressing. All this attention is rooted in what she calls the "sacred vulnerability" of our bodies. Even aside from issues of sex and sexuality, Paulsell claims that at the heart of Christian care for the poor and marginalized is affirmation of the goodness of the body: "Christian conviction about the goodness of the body, coupled with a recognition of the body's vulnerabilities, has nurtured a profound sense of responsibility for the protection and nourishment of bodies throughout the history of the church."[11] That Christians are called to the care of more than simply the soul of an individual is a testament to the value of our bodies in the eyes of God, regardless of the appearance or identity of those bodies.

One source of wisdom regarding a positive sense of incarnation and embodiment comes from our trans siblings. In his book *Transformed: The Bible and the Lives of Trans Christians,* Austin Hartke affirms his belief in the sacred intention of his trans identity: "I don't believe God made a mistake in creating me just as I am. God created me with a body that was designated female when I was born—a body I struggled to connect with for the first twenty-six years of my life and that I now finally feel at home in . . . I think God made me transgender on purpose."[12] An affirmation of incarnation as a signal of the goodness of our bodies points us toward the experience of being at home in our bodies. We are not spiritual strangers temporarily taking up residence in our bodies like travelers visiting a hostel. We are meant to own, experience, and celebrate our bodies as an essential part of our identity as God's beloved creation. This is tricky to navigate when the body we see does not reflect how we identify, or when we feel as though our bodies are betraying us through aging or disease. But if the bodily resurrection of Jesus Christ proves anything, it shows us the value God puts on our bodies and the lengths to which God will go to save them.

AN ETHIC OF SEXUAL WHOLENESS

Sexual wholeness begins by affirming the goodness of desires, as revealed in Creation, and the goodness of our bodies, as revealed in the Incarnation. That leads to the question: What does this look like in practice?

A positive ethic of Christian sexual wholeness recognizes that desire originates from and is properly and most completely fulfilled by God. It also affirms the goodness of our bodies as divine assets and deeply valuable to God. Furthermore, it affirms that, as with anything good, both our desire and our bodies can be used for evil. We see it in unwanted sexual contact and when sex occurs across power differences or in other examples of "asymmetrical" sexual practices such as rape, pedophilia, and bestiality.[13] It also affirms that sex can occur outside of the expansive depth and breadth of meaning sexual wholeness would suggest.

With all of that, a positive ethic of Christian sexual wholeness affirms that the fullest expression of the sexual experience occurs over time and in the context of a stable, covenant relationship. It's in such a relationship that we can experience the depth of desire, the risk and practice of vulnerability, the safety provided by the covenant itself, and the longevity that allows each person to be fully celebrated through all of life's changes.

It doesn't take a rocket scientist to figure out that sex often occurs outside of a long-term, covenant relationship. A lot. But what if an ethic of Christian sexual wholeness allowed for this and could even be informed by this? Instead of dismissing this experience of intimacy or release of biological tension, what if Christian sexual wholeness stretches the conversation beyond what we expect and invites us to consider something more? Paulsell writes,

> "Sex between people who do not love one another and are not willing to become uniquely responsible to and for one another assumes a split between body and spirit that does not exist. When we have sex, all of who we are is on the line. Any attempt to deploy our bodies in a sexual encounter while holding back the rest of our selves damages us; the impossible attempt to divide body and spirit does violence to both."[14]

A positive ethic of Christian sexual wholeness doesn't have to offer a flat "no" to sex without marriage, but it does offer a caution against the cavalier treatment of sex, something that can happen inside a long-term relationship or marriage as easily as outside of it. If our bodies matter to God and if desire originates from God, then how we use our bodies to experience desire should matter deeply to us.

Our bodies are made in the image of God and are capable of bearing divinity. Desire originates in God and finds its ultimate fulfilment in God. Holding these two concepts together allows us to exist in the world as fully integrated beings, capable of experiencing, but not being overwhelmed by or captive to, embodied desires. Maybe the best way of thinking about sexual wholeness is to think of freedom. As fully-integrated, self-aware beings, we are free to experience embodied desire, but we also have to protect that freedom from being overwhelmed by that desire.

Sexual wholeness recognizes that we desire to touch and be touched, to see and be seen, to affirm and be affirmed. It's a realization that our bodies aren't barriers to experiencing the divine, but tools to facilitate that connection to God and through one another. I think this is the conversation I yearned for as a child, although I certainly wasn't aware of it. It was this: God desires us and so God made us. Within each of us, God placed desire so that we might desire connection—with one another and ultimately with God. Sex is not simply a biological urge; rather, it is a special expression of a desire that lives deep within us and should be treated as such. We have the freedom to make choices about sex, but never to make a choice that takes away another's choice. Sex will be awkward, and clumsy, and probably really embarrassing sometimes, if we choose to love and be loved by another and to express that love physically. But over time, each of us and those we call beloved will learn to celebrate the awkward, clumsy, and embarrassing moments as the continual unfolding of our love for one another, always bearing in mind how much each of us is desired by God.

Rev. Marcus Halley is a 2015 Master of Sacred Theology graduate and current Doctor of Ministry in Preaching student at the School of Theology at the University of the South. He currently serves as the eighteenth Rector of Saint Paul's Church on Lake of the Isles in Minneapolis, Minnesota. His primary theological interests include evangelism, liturgy, formation, and mission. Outside of Saint Paul's Church, Marcus speaks and facilitates conversations around the intersection of race, sexuality, and faith. His work has appeared on Grow Christians, The Logos Project, Lent Madness, Forward Day-by-Day, and Thirty Seconds or Less.

ENDNOTES

1   Wil Gafney. *Womanist Midrash: A Reintroduction to the Woman of the Torah and the Throne* (Louisville: Westminster John Knox Press, 2017), 4.

2   Augustine of Hippo, *Book 1,* trans. John K. Ryan (New York: Doubleday Books, 1960), 19.

3   Hildegard of Bingen, quoted in *Women Writers of the Middle Ages,* Peter Dronke (Cambridge: Cambridge University Press, 1984), 175.

4   Rachel Held Evans, *Inspired: Walking on Water, Slaying Dragons, and Leaning to Love the Bible Again* (Nashville: Thomas Nelson, 2018), 203.

5   Rowan Williams, "The Body's Grace" (Tenth Michael Harding Memorial Address delivered to the Lesbian and Gay Christian Movement, London, 1989).

6   Audre Lorde, "Uses of the Erotic," from in *Sister Outsider (Freedom, CA: The Crossing Press, 2007) 56.*

7   Williams.

8   Ibid.

9   Augustine, *Confessions, (Cambridge, MA: Hackett Publishing, 2006),* Chapter 12, no. 18.

10   Stephanie Paulsell, *Honoring the Body: Meditations on a Christian Practice* (San Francisco: John Wiley & Sons, 2002), 8.

11   Paulsell, 13.

12   Austin Hartke, *Transformed: The Bible & the Lives of Transgender Christians* (Louisville: Westminster John Knox Press, 2018), 2.

13   Williams.

14   Paulsell, 157.

MORE RESOURCES ON SEXUALITY

ONLINE RESOURCES:

"I've Lived As A Man And A Woman: Here's What I Learned,"
TEDxMileHigh Wonder Event by Paula Stone Williams
>www.youtube.com

GLAAD
>www.glaad.org

National Center for Transgender Equality
>www.transequality.org

Q Christian Fellowship
>www.qchristian.org

The Genderbread Person
>www.itspronouncedmetrosexual.com/2015/03/
>the-genderbread-person-v3

NON-FICTION

Unprotected Texts: The Bible's Surprising Contradictions about Sex and Desire
>By Jennifer Wright Knust

Transforming: The Bible and the Lives of Transgender Christians
>By Austen Hartke

Bible, Gender, Sexuality: Reframing the Church's Debate on Same-Sex Relationships
>By James V. Brownson

Undivided: Coming Out, Becoming Whole, and Living Free from Shame
By Vicky Beeching

Sexuality and the Black Church: A Womanist Perspective
By Kelly B. Douglas

I Thought It Was Just Me (But It Isn't): Making the Journey from "What Will People Think?" to "I Am Enough"
By Brené Brown

Rising Strong: How the Ability to Reset Transforms the Way We Live, Love, Parent, and Lead
By Brené Brown

Purity Myth: How America's Obsession with Virginity is Hurting Young Women
By Jessica Valenti

She's My Dad: A Father's Transition and a Son's Redemption
by Jonathan Williams, with Paula Stone Williams

Come As You Are: The Surprising New Science that Will Transform Your Sex Life.
By Emily Negoski

The Heart and Soul of Sex: Exploring the Sexual Mysteries
By Gina Ogden

Girls & Sex: Navigating the Complicated New Landscape
By Peggy Orienstein

The Heart of Desire: Keys to the Pleasures of Love
By Stella Resnick

Sex, God, and the Conservative Church: Erasing Shame from Sexual Intimacy
By Tina Schermer Sellers

Boy Erased: A Memoir of Identity, Faith, and Family
  By Garrard Conley

Transgender History (2nd Ed.): The Roots of Today's Revolution
  By Susan Stryker

The Descent of Man
  By Grayson Perry

Damaged Goods: New Perspectives on Christian Purity
  By Dianna E. Anderson

Queer Virtue: What LGBTQ People Know About Life and Love and How It Can Revitalize Christianity
  By Rev. Elizabeth M. Edman

The Gender Knot: Unraveling our Patriarchal Legacy
  By Allan G. Johnson

Torn: Rescuing the Gospel from the Gays-vs.-Christians Debate
  By Justin Lee

Quiverfull: Inside the Christian Patriarchy Movement
  By Kathryn Joyce